W9-ANC-778

New World

SOURDOUGH

New World

SOURD

Artisan Techniques *for* Creative Homemade
Fermented Breads

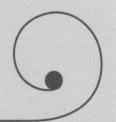

OUGH

WITH RECIPES FOR BIROTE, BAGELS,
PAN DE COCO, BEIGNETS, AND MORE

Bryan Ford

Founder of ArtisanBryan.com

QUARRY

Brimming with creative inspiration, how-to projects, and useful information to enrich your everyday life, Quarto Knows is a favorite destination for those pursuing their interests and passions. Visit our site and dig deeper with our books into your area of interest: Quarto Creates, Quarto Cooks, Quarto Homes, Quarto Lives, Quarto Drives, Quarto Explores, Quarto Gifts, or Quarto Kids.

© 2020 Quarto Publishing Group USA Inc.
Text © 2020 Bryan Ford

First Published in 2020 by Quarry Books, an imprint of The Quarto Group,
100 Cummings Center, Suite 265-D, Beverly, MA 01915, USA.
T (978) 282-9590 F (978) 283-2742 QuartoKnows.com

All rights reserved. No part of this book may be reproduced in any form without written permission of the copyright owners. All images in this book have been reproduced with the knowledge and prior consent of the artists concerned, and no responsibility is accepted by producer, publisher, or printer for any infringement of copyright or otherwise, arising from the contents of this publication. Every effort has been made to ensure that credits accurately comply with information supplied. We apologize for any inaccuracies that may have occurred and will resolve inaccurate or missing information in a subsequent reprinting of the book.

Quarry Books titles are also available at discount for retail, wholesale, promotional, and bulk purchase. For details, contact the Special Sales Manager by email at specialsales@quarto.com or by mail at The Quarto Group, Attn: Special Sales Manager, 100 Cummings Center, Suite 265-D, Beverly, MA 01915, USA.

10 9 8 7 6

ISBN: 978-1-63159-870-8

Digital edition published in 2020
eISBN: 978-1-63159-871-5

Ford, Bryan, author.
New world sourdough : artisan techniques for creative homemade fermented breads; with recipes for birote, bagels, pan de coco, beignets and more / Bryan Ford.
ISBN 9781631598708 (hardcover) | ISBN 9781631598715 (ebook)
1. Cooking (Sourdough) 2. Sourdough bread. 3. Fermentation. 4. Cookbooks.
LCC TX770.S66 F67 2012 (print) | LCC TX770.S66 (ebook) | DDC 641.81/5--dc23

LCCN 2020000169 (print) | LCCN 2020000170 (ebook)

Design: Tanya Jacobson, jcbsn.co
Photography: Stephanie Lynn Warga

Printed in China

Dedication

This book is dedicated to my *family*
and *friends*, for loving me and
supporting my journey as a baker.

PART II

Recipes, *page 39*

Ch. 2 | Rustic Breads, page 41

Ch. 3 | Enriched Sourdough Breads, page 97

INTRODUCTION

What Bread Baking Means to Me

Baking bread. Those two words, together, take me to a different world. A world of creativity. A world of passion. But, if you have ever read my blog, you'll know that the most important world those words bring me to is the world my parents are from. My roots. My parents were born and raised in Honduras. My father is an Afro-Honduran from La Ceiba, where African slaves were brought to work on banana plantations, among other forms of labor. My mother is from San Pedro Sula, where the indigenous Mayan people were conquered by the Spanish, who were completing their final voyage to the New World.

Although my parents initially imigrated to New York City in the 1980s and I was born in the Bronx, we promptly relocated to New Orleans. My parents saw opportunity there due to its existing Honduran population. In the early 1900s the banana trade took many Hondurans to New Orleans and created the largest population of Hondurans in the United States (though my birthplace, the Bronx, may have something to say about that). New Orleans became my home and I grew up eating the best of both worlds.

At home, Honduran cuisine was the norm. I watched my mother knead tortilla masa, or dough, time and again. I could tell that the process of making tortillas was a methodical and meditative one. Not too much flour, she would tell me, as the dough would be too dry. The key to a good *tortilla hondurena* is coconut milk, she would say. You need to find the right balance between the amounts of coconut milk, water, and oil. I listened and watched—waiting for my chance to, one day, take part in this tradition. To make *baleadas*, the tortillas are filled with creamy red beans, *crema* (cream), and *queso fresco hondureno* (fresh Honduran cheese). In New Orleans, this cheese is, thankfully, readily available. For dessert she would always treat the family to *pastelitos de piña*. These pineapple jam–filled hand pies were always gone before they had a chance to cool. If it wasn't that for dessert, my dad would come home with a fresh bag of *semitas* or *pan de coco*, which would be perfect for afternoon coffee on the porch and for the *wirros* (Honduran slang for "kids") to have with milk. I always knew Honduran bread was special and delicious and I am so happy that I not only make it regularly, but can also share parts of it with you.

Combined with these traditions is my experience as a line cook in New Orleans. When added together you get Artisan Bryan. I bake because—like New Orleans—it's fun and shouldn't be taken too seriously. Your environment dictates the bread you can create—and I'm not talking about climate and temperature. I'm talking about how you feel and the emotional connection you have to your roots, upbringing, and city. It is said that when you bake bread, your emotions show in the dough and the final bread. I've always found this to be true—but it's time to take that a step further. I find that when you allow yourself to be free of judgment and expectation, you will find a greater appreciation and satisfaction in the bread you make with your own two hands.

Take a moment to remember that to achieve certain characteristics in bread you must start from scratch. That means you must accept that it will take some time to cultivate your craft and acquire knowledge. Make sure you balance your expectation for perfection with an appreciation of the processes, showing satisfaction with yourself and your bread every step of the way. Here are two philosophies I carry with me as I have progressed from home baker to head baker and bakery consultant.

Be Understanding.

Understand that there really are no rules or boundaries in baking. Learn to embrace your instincts, emotions, and passion. Most importantly, understand that it takes a lot of time and practice to achieve certain aesthetic traits in your bread.

Take Your Time.

Consistency and perfection are not bad goals to have! But they take time—and you should take every second of it. Cherish the moments of struggle and experimentation as you watch them turn into predictable and reliable forms of baking bread. Trust me, even the most seasoned bakers deal with the fluctuation of many variables every day. What does this mean? That you will always need to have patience to achieve your bread goals. If you stick with the process and use your passion to cultivate your craft, you will get the results you seek.

What Is New World Sourdough?

Whether you are a home baker or a professional, this is a great time to be a *new world* sourdough bread baker. The internet and social media, like in most industries, has made detailed information about the craft readily available. But, how much is too much? Should a brand-new baker be worried about hydration levels and crumb structures? I learned how to bake long before I had an Instagram or Facebook account and it was out of curiosity, pleasure, and necessity. My dad really liked cinnamon-raisin bagels from the store, so, when I was a *wirro*, I learned to make a cinnamon-raisin bread for him. It was pure imagination, not with the goal to make a bread with a certain type of crumb structure, but to make something to please and nourish my loved ones. He even liked it when I didn't grease the loaf tin and burned the loaves to a crisp. And although my mother's tortillas had the perfect flavor and shape every time, she never used a recipe. They weren't perfect because she, initially, sought to make perfect tortillas. Her mastery of the craft came simply through repetition and using her instincts as her guide. Her tips and tricks to kneading the perfect masa are hilariously unorthodox, such as oiling a cutting board and putting it diagonally in the sink to get the right angle to *amasar*, or knead. Although I won't get into the whole history of bread, I can't imagine that, for the thousands of years in which bread has been baked, the end goal of a perfect crumb structure and aesthetics dominated the conversations between the village miller and baker.

Speaking of aesthetics, what is it that makes a sourdough bread distinctly a *sourdough* bread? At grocery stores I always find it interesting to see packaged loaves labeled "San Francisco" sourdough. Most people equate the word sourdough with a certain flavor profile and appearance. Although I do enjoy a nice, crusty loaf of sour bread, I perceive sourdough as simply a means to make different kinds of bread rise in a healthier and more natural way. In Honduras, a traditional pan de coco was not even leavened. As the coasts were abundant with coconuts, the meat and water from the coconut were mixed with flour and water and baked in stone ovens. Before the introduction of commercial yeast, one can imagine that the beginning of wild yeast and natural leavening occurred unintentionally and instinctually in the baking process. If you let a flour and water mixture sit long enough, it will ferment—especially in a tropical climate. A dense loaf of pan de coco is no less "sourdough" than a crunchy batard with an open, light crumb.

My intentions for writing this book are not only to share my recipes and stories with you, but also to embrace a more simplified bread-making process that celebrates creative approaches to flavor while appreciating the quality of every single loaf that comes out of the oven. Your hands are powerful tools, eager to learn new things. I want you to use this book and feel inspired to create and explore. I want you to lose your expectations of bread. I want you to see baking differently. I want you to understand yourself better. I want you to enter a new world.

PART I

Sourdough Techniques

Ah, technique. The physical execution of an art form. The building blocks to craftsman-ship. It's easy to get lost in the world of studying techniques and hoping, one day, to master them. It's also just as easy to become overwhelmed by the thought of needing specialized equipment or ingredients to learn those techniques. Rest assured, you can cultivate the craft of baking sourdough bread in a simple, straightforward, and minimalistic approach in your own home.

Because of the importance of building your bread-making knowledge base, I include this part of the book to serve as a step-by-step guide to the things you need to know to start baking my delicious bread recipes! You will need a few tools for your kitchen (do not worry; I encourage a lot of improvisation). After you have your gear, I will review the staple ingre-dients you will need to stock your kitchen. Once your kitchen and cabinets are stocked, the real fun begins with the creation of your sourdough starter and a review of the techniques used in each step of the baking process. The first technique, and recipe, covered in this section is the most important one: building a sourdough starter completely from scratch. Building your very own starter, especially if it is your first one, can feel stressful. Remember to relax because with time, patience, and love your starter will come out working and tasting beautifully.

1

TOOLS, INGREDIENTS, AND TECHNIQUES

In each recipe I give you the techniques, tools, and ingredients I use when making that particular bread and I will refer you back to this section for detailed explanations, as needed. I recommend you use these techniques and methods for each recipe at least once. As you become more comfortable with sourdough baking, get creative and make modifications. For example, if my recipe says to shape with a tension roll and bake in a cast iron vessel, it is perfectly acceptable to use the rounding technique and bake it on a sheet pan instead. Use this section as a guide and just remember, in the real world, your situation, environment, and dough will be different. I love seeing people use my blog and making their own modifications to some parts of the process after they have tried the recipe a few times. Baking shouldn't cause stress, so if your technique doesn't match mine exactly every time you go through the process, rest assured it's all good! You will always achieve your goal of making delicious bread.

Tools

Here are the tools I encourage you to have in your kitchen so you can bake like a champ. I also include any possible improvisations you can use.

Kitchen scale: Your scale will be your best friend while using this book. All ingredients for all recipes in this book are measured in grams—even the liquids—because it is much easier to bake consistently when you weigh your ingredients. I prefer a digital scale so you clearly can see each gram weighed, which is important for items called for in smaller quantities, like salt or vanilla.

Bowls and jars: It's important to have a few different mixing bowls in your kitchen so you can measure and combine ingredients separately, if needed. I'm also a fan of mixing dough in one bowl and then transferring it to another bowl for the initial rise time. Any material (metal, plastic, glass) will do, as long as the bowl is big enough to handle the increase in dough size. It is also important to have a few bowls and jars with lids to maintain your sourdough starter.

Dough/bench scraper: Having one of these tools is helpful when cutting and dividing dough, especially as you become more experienced and make larger quantities of dough. However, any chef's knife, or your hands, will do to get you started.

Proofing vessels: There are many ways to proof bread (see page 32 for more on this). The most popular way is to use bannetons, which are wooden baskets that come in different shapes and sizes. These can be pricey. I prefer to use any bowl or loaf tin lined with a clean kitchen towel, or just allow my dough to proof on a cutting board dusted with semolina. Another popular item used for proofing is a baker's couche, which is a cloth traditionally made with linen. Again, you can improvise here with a clean kitchen towel dusted with whole-wheat and rice flours.

Baking vessels: You will need baking (loaf) tins: 2¾ × 4½ × 8½-inch (7 × 11 × 21 cm), a high quality pizza stone, and a cast iron Dutch oven. You will also need a half sheet pan or two (13 × 18-inch, or 45 × 33 cm).

Ingredients

Basic bread ingredients are simple. To be prepared for any baking urges that hit, keep your pantry stocked with the following items.

Flour

There are many different types of flour available all over the world, which is exciting to me. I aspire to travel and taste as many different grains as possible! For the purposes of this book, you will only need a few types of flour that can be found at your local grocery store.

All-Purpose Flour

Although there is quite a bit of protein in all-purpose flour, it is less than bread (strong) flour and, thus, can be used for a variety of things, such as cookies and cakes. I like to use more all-purpose flour in the Enriched Sourdough Breads chapter (see page 97) to ensure as soft and delicate an interior as possible.

Bread Flour/Strong Flour

This flour has a higher protein content than all-purpose flour, which means it can create more strands of gluten in the dough. You will see a lot more of this ingredient in the Rustic Breads chapter (see page 41) as it gives your loaves more volume (height) and chew.

Gluten-Free Flours

I occasionally use oat, rice, and coconut flour to add flavor and softness to some breads. However, if you do not have these flours on hand, simply use all-purpose, gluten-free flour in its place.

Rye Flour

Rye is a grain, similar to wheat, but with a significantly lower protein content. It's a very healthy and flavorful flour to use and is beneficial to making a sourdough starter from scratch because of all the nutrients in the berry.

Spelt Flour

Throughout the book you will see that I like to add small percentages of spelt flour to some mixes. Spelt is an ancient grain with a nutty flavor and it provides a touch of airiness to any dough. It is also a healthy, easily digestible grain. If you can't find spelt for one of the recipes, it's okay. Simply replace any spelt called for with all-purpose flour, whole-wheat flour, or a combination of the two.

Whole-Wheat Flour

You may be surprised to learn that, although whole-wheat flour has a higher protein content, gluten development is substantially weaker in this type of flour. Whole-wheat flour is milled to include the entirety of the wheat berry, and the bran and germ components carry with them a different type of protein than the gluten-developing type. However, these wheat berry components makes using whole-wheat flour a very healthy option when baking.

Water

Water is the second most important ingredient in the baking process. I typically use water straight from the tap at home with no issues. However, be aware that elevated chlorine levels in your water can impede fermentation. Filtered water is always a great choice if chlorine is an issue. For my mixing and starter creation, I will tell you to use "warm" water, which is water that is not hot or steamy—it's somewhere between 80°F and 90°F (26.6°C to 32.2°C). Other times, I will say to use room temperature water in a recipe—that is somewhere between 70°F and 75°F (21°C to 24°C). I recommend using a thermometer once or twice to get a good feel for these temperature ranges, but don't worry about it every time you need water. You will develop an instinct for when to use warmer or cooler water as you bake more—on a hot day in your kitchen, you can use cooler water. On a cold day, use warmer water, etc.

Salt

My cabinet is always stocked with kosher and sea salts for my sourdough bread baking. I recommend using either of these, but I also use some odd salts, such as ghost pepper salt and Himalayan pink salt at times.

Wild Yeast

Your sourdough starter is going to cultivate wild yeasts from the air and, over time, will make your bread rise. This sourdough starter is the leavening agent on your ingredient list.

Enrichers

For a dough to be enriched, it needs to include some sort of fat, sugar, eggs, milk, or a combination of these things. I will, typically, call for unsalted butter, coconut oil, or olive oil but feel free to use these ingredients interchangeably, as you prefer. I have never had an issue replacing or substituting fats in a recipe.

For sugar, I like to use brown sugar, honey, or granulated white sugar. I don't consider a bread to be enriched if it includes only a small amount of one or two of these components and still maintains the look and texture of a rustic bread—like a focaccia or the Olive Oil and Sea Salt Tin Loaf (page 47), for example.

Techniques

Get ready! Here you'll learn all about making that all-important, and all-personal of ingredients, your sourdough starter. Once you master that, it's all about mixing, shaping, proofing, and baking. Are you ready?

Making and Maintaining Your Sourdough Starter

Before you begin, it is important to point out that you can make a sourdough starter with any of the flours listed in the ingredients section (see page 17). My preference is to use 100 percent rye flour, which, during some parts of the year when it is a bit hotter, produces a fully ripe and ready-to-go starter in just 3 days. Typically, however, making an active starter takes 5 to 7 days before you see the type of activity necessary to make your bread rise, especially if you are using all-purpose or bread flour to start this process. I strongly recommend using at least some rye or whole-wheat flour, though, because the nutrients these flours carry with them will ensure the success of your starter creation—not to mention they are much more flavorful. So, for the purposes of my technique, we will use 100 percent rye flour.

Without a doubt, this is the most important technique you will need to master to make the recipes in this book. Fortunately, I like to think of this as one of the easiest things you can possibly do. It requires nothing but a few minutes a day and a warm-ish spot in your kitchen.

To get started, you need rye flour, warm water, a fork, and a jar. I prefer to use a tall jar (glass or plastic) with a cover, because this allows you to see growth in your starter during days 3 through 5. The mixture needs to sit for 24 hours between feedings, so pick a time of day that fits your schedule every day for one week—right when you wake up or right before bedtime are usually good bets, so you do not miss one in the middle of the day.

Keep your climate in mind around days 3 through 5. When I lived in warm tropical climates, my starter quickly showed signs of activity and growth and was ready to make bread in 3 days. I recommend reading the daily descriptions on page 22 before you start so you understand what will occur during the starter building process. That way, if things are moving fast, you will recognize the characteristics. Conversely, if you are in a cooler climate and things are progressing more slowly, you can recognize that it may take a little more time to see the starter characteristics developing.

Making Your Starter: Day 1

The first day of starter making is the most relaxing of them all. In a tall jar with a lid, simply mix 100 grams of rye flour with 100 grams of warm water. Use a fork to mix the ingredients well, ensuring no dry flour remains. Keep this in an environment between 70°F and 80°F (21°C and 26.6°C). Again, become familiar with the exact temperature if you need to and try to develop your instincts as you move forward. You can get a kitchen thermometer for exact temperature readings and make a log at each feeding. Every kitchen will have different hot spots, especially in varying climates. The top of the fridge or near the stove is always a good bet for a warm place. You won't get much of a funky smell after this mix, as the flour is fresh and has not fermented yet.

Making Your Starter: Day 2

Twenty-four hours after combining the flour and water, you will notice some tiny bubbles in the mixture. You shouldn't see much, if any, growth in volume, but it is possible to see some if you live in a hot climate or have a more elevated ambient temperature in your kitchen.

When you open the container, you will notice a smell that may not be so pleasant. This is normal. Weigh and keep 100 grams of your starter, discarding the rest. Because your starter is not fully mature yet, you aren't going to find much use for the excess because the flavor and texture are simply not yet desirable.

You will now feed the reserved starter: add 100 grams of rye flour and 100 grams of lukewarm water. Mix with a fork until the mixture is evenly combined and there is no dry flour remaining. You want your starter to maintain a slight thickness in the consistency, so always check to make sure your mixture isn't too wet. You can tell it is too wet if it becomes very thin and almost watery. If you tilt the container and it runs very quickly, it may be a bit overhydrated. If your mixture does get too wet, no worries. For the next feeding, use a little less water. Close the lid, and place the container back in the same warm place for another 24 hours.

Making Your Starter: Days 3 and 4

On both the third and fourth day, follow the routine: Weigh and keep 100 grams of the starter mixture, discarding the rest. Feed the starter 100 grams of rye flour and 100 grams of lukewarm water. Close the lid and return the container to its spot for another 24 hours.

On these days you will start to notice a slightly sweet and acidic smell from your mixture. In addition to this, you should see a noticeable increase in the size of the bubbles present. It will look a bit grainy as well.

If you are using a tall jar, you will see signs that your starter has risen and fallen. These are all good signs of activity in your new starter.

Making Your Starter: Day 5

It is very likely that later on day 5 your starter will be active and ready to build a levain for mixing your sourdough breads (more info on this follows; see page 24). After you feed your starter, place a rubber band or other marker on your jar at the level of your starter to monitor the predictability of its rise and fall. You want to mark the level after feeding because a simple test of an active sourdough starter is the predictability of its cycle. This rise and fall indicates which stage your starter is in: When you see signs of growth on the sides of your jar but the actual starter level is lower than the starter residue markings on the sides of the jar, it means your starter is ripe, mature, and past its peak. If you see your starter significantly risen above your marking, possibly more than doubled in size, this stage is considered peak.

When it is past its peak and mature, you will smell a very strong, but pleasant, acidic aroma. The mixture will be soft to the touch with a weblike texture that breaks easily when you tear at it with your fingers. When the starter is doubled in size and at peak, you will smell a slightly sweeter aroma and, if you pull at it, it will be relatively strong. Keep in mind that because you are using rye flour at this stage, the structure in your starter will not be as strong as later when you build it using white and whole-wheat flours.

At this stage it is worth keeping some of the excess starter as a back-up, or for use in things such as piecrusts and pancakes, and, of course, for the day you accidentally throw all your active starter away! You can refrigerate the excess, according to the maintenance steps following.

Before we begin building our levain for making bread, here are two ways you can maintain and store your brand new sourdough starter.

Maintaining Your Starter: Method 1—Once a Day, Ambient Temperature

Once you are past the point of building your starter and it is healthy and performs consistently as indicated by a predictable rise and fall after feedings, I recommend you feed your starter once a day, at ambient/room temperature. This allows you to become familiar with how your starter looks when it is ready for building a levain, or adding to your final mix. Note that for maintenance you can use flour other than rye; however, you are also more than welcome to continue using just rye flour. One good approach is to use half rye and half whole-wheat flour to balance the flavor. If your schedule can afford it, twice-a-day feedings (roughly every 12 hours) keep your starter extremely active and healthy. However, do not stress if there is no time to feed this often. Once a day has worked just fine for me.

Maintaining Your Starter: Method 2—Once a Week, Fridge

The best time to refrigerate your starter, if you do not plan to bake every day, is right after a feeding. When you are ready to use it, take it out of the fridge and let it rest at room temperature for about 8 hours; and then it will be ready for your levain build. Depending on your fridge temperature, it may be ready to use as soon as you take it out of the fridge. Try to take note of any marks that would indicate that the starter rose and subsequently fell.

Building and Maintaining a Levain

So, you must be wondering: What is a levain? As mentioned in Making Your Starter: Day 5 (page 23), when your starter reaches its peak and doubles in size after a feeding, it is ready to make bread rise, and is called a levain. Every time you want to make a sourdough bread recipe, the first step to each recipe is to feed some mature starter with flour and water. This is the levain build. Keep in mind that because you will always need mature starter to keep this process going, you may want to make more than you actually need so you always have extra starter after the levain goes past its peak and dwindles into a mature starter.

Some people keep their brand new separate starter, feeding it in a way that suits their needs (once a day, twice a day, once a week, etc.), and then pull out the amount they need for a specific levain build for a recipe. Here are the methods you can use to maintain your starter and build levains, as well as an example to help you understand the process.

Building a Levain/Maintaining Your Starter: Method 1

My sourdough starter is mature on day 5. I'm going to feed it rye flour once a day to keep it healthy, but I'm also going to take some of it to build a levain for a recipe mix. This allows me to keep the strong rye flavor profile in the starter, but use more mellow-flavored flours (such as bread flour or whole-wheat flour) in my dough mix.

Building a Levain/Maintaining Your Starter: Method 2

My sourdough starter is mature, fed, and in the fridge. I take it out a few days later and let it come to room temperature. It has since matured again, so I use some of it to build a separate levain and I also refresh the starter itself so it can go back into the fridge.

Building a Levain/Maintaining Your Starter: Method 3

This is the method I always use. I feed my starter once or twice a day and use it as my levain for my dough mixes. I make sure there is extra built into my feeding so the excess of what I need for the mix can mature past the point of leavening bread and be fed again. Here is how this works:

- 100 g mature starter (from day 5, past its peak and mature.)
- 200 g bread flour
- 180 g water

In a medium bowl, mix the ingredients well. Cover the bowl and let it sit at room temperature for 3 to 4 hours. It is then ready to use for making bread. However, I intentionally make more than needed in the recipe so the rest can continue to mature to the point where it needs to be fed again. That excess has, thus, remained my starter. If I don't plan to bake again, I'll feed it some rye or whole-wheat flour to maintain it throughout the next day. From there, I can continue to build levains for baking or maintain the starter, as needed.

This example build is 480 grams of levain (note that most times you will end up a bit short; this is also a good reason to build a little extra levain). After I use 350 grams in a recipe, I can leave the remaining amount in the container and feed it again once it gets to the maturity point (usually between 12 and 24 hours).

So, to recap, I used 350 grams of levain 4 hours after feeding it and the remaining amount was fed again 12 to 24 hours later.

In each recipe, I will give you the levain build that works best for that specific recipe. It does not matter which of the preceding methods you use to maintain your starter, so long as you make the build for each recipe.

Slowly adding water to the mix.

Adding salt and water after resting the initial mix.

Mixing Dough

Mixing: Final Rustic Dough (Non-Enriched Breads)

Final dough mixing means you have a levain ready to be used and you want to mix it with the other ingredients needed to make the bread. For breads that are not enriched, meaning there is no added fat or sugar (think rustic loaves, the old "flour, water, yeast, salt"–type breads), mixing the dough is a pretty relaxing process. You, once again, need only your hands, a bowl, and a clean work surface.

When you are hand-mixing dough, the key is to accept that you might make a mess and have sticky hands. It's okay! The more times you get your hands in the dough, the more you will learn about why it feels the way it does at certain stages. Here is my go-to mixing method for rustic breads, for which you can find the recipes in chapter 2.

Mixing Dough: Method 1—Non-Enriched Breads

- Take about 75 percent of the total water called for in the final dough mix and dissolve your levain into it.

- Add all the flour and mix by squeezing the dough until the water gets absorbed.

- Over the course of 5 to 10 minutes, slowly add most of the remaining water; you're saving a tiny bit for when we add the salt. Make sure you squeeze the dough, but do not tear it, to help the water absorb.

- Once the dough absorbs all the water, let it sit for about 20 minutes to let the gluten structure begin developing. Keep in mind that fermentation has started because the levain has been added.

- Add the salt and some of the remaining water. Squeeze it into the dough for about 5 minutes, or until everything is absorbed and the dough has a smooth-ish surface.

- Add the last bit of water and repeat the squeezing process.

Squeezing all the ingredients together.

Kneading the dough with the palm of the hand.

Follow the recipe instructions after you've finished mixing, as each recipe will have a protocol for anything different you may need to do to the dough during the first rise.

Mixing: Final Dough (Enriched and Some Non-Enriched Rustic Breads)

I mix my enriched doughs differently than most rustic doughs. Why? Generally, because they have a much lower hydration and it is easier to incorporate everything at once without ending up with a soup (except the brioche, which is best done with a stand mixer!). However, some of the rustic breads recipes have a lower hydration and it makes more sense to use this method as well. Pay attention to the type of fat in the recipe and the type of consistency the bread should have. I have never had a problem using fats interchangeably, so if you don't want to use butter, substitute any type of oil into your mix instead.

Mixing Dough: Method 2—Enriched Breads and Some Non-Enriched Rustic Breads

For an enriched dough recipe, combine the ingredients in a medium bowl. Using your hands, squeeze everything together and then turn the dough out onto a work surface. Knead the dough using the palm of your hand to push it forward, and then your fingers to pull it back toward your hand. Repeat this process until you have a smooth surface. Don't be afraid to rip this dough while you knead with your palm and then bring it back together again.

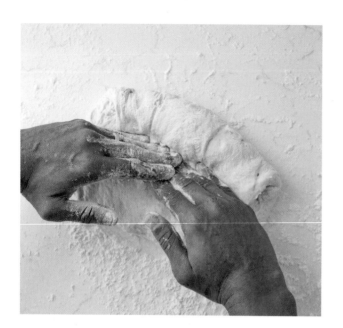 

Shaping Dough

There are many ways to shape dough. I outline my favorite techniques here and I reference which ones you should use in a recipe, as needed. Note: When shaping dough requires a floured work surface, I typically use whatever flour is available, but all-purpose flour is preferable.

Shaping Dough: Method 1—Tension Roll

My go-to shaping for most loaves is the tension roll. This type of shape works well if you are using a banneton, loaf tin, couche, kitchen towel, or cutting board as your proofing method.

Flour a work surface if you feel that the dough is too sticky or too difficult to shape. There is no amount of flour that can be too little or too much—do what works for the work surface and your ability to deal with the dough.

- Pat down the dough into a narrow square or rectangle.

- Use your pinky fingers to pull the dough into itself and then push outward to create tension.

- Repeat this process until the dough is rolled tightly. If the dough is not rolled tightly enough, use the palm of your hand to gently pat down the seam and seal it.

Shaping Dough: Method 2—Rounding

Rounding dough is helpful if you want to proof it in a bowl or other spherical vessel to make a round loaf of bread. Simply pat the dough piece you are working down flat. Take two opposing corners and bring them to the middle. Take the other two corners and do the same. You can repeat this until the dough is too tight and there are no more corners. Flip the dough upside-down and use the palm of your hands, on the side of the dough, to tighten the dough gently with a circular motion. Make sure you don't tear the dough on the surface, as this will affect the quality of the baked bread.

Shaping Dough: Method 3—Balling Up

I refer to making small balls of dough as "balling up" the dough. This is great for shaping smaller types of bread that either need to be baked as small, rounded dough balls or pre-shaped into these balls and then stretched out (like for pizza crust and tortillas).

When you divide the dough, on a lightly floured surface (note here that too much flour may make it impossible to create tension in the ball of dough), gently pat the dough pieces down. Fold the corners into the middle, similar to the rounding technique (see page 30) but on a smaller scale, and flip the dough over. Now, use the palm of your hand and your fingers to roll the ball back and forth until you have a small ball of dough and a smooth surface. Do not let the surface of the dough tear, which means you have shaped it too tightly. If you don't want to waste the torn dough, let it rest for a while and try to shape it again.

Proofing Dough

Proofing dough is necessary for your bread to get an additional rise after it has been shaped, but before it goes into the oven. No matter the vessel you choose to proof the dough, you want your shaped dough to remain in a covered environment so it does not develop a dry skin from the air.

When the dough enters the proofing stage directly after shaping, you will notice it has a smooth surface and forms a tight loaf that does not jiggle much and is tough to the touch.

After the dough is proofed, you will notice the loaf may be bubbly and has a spring to it when touched with your finger. It will also have a nice wiggle to it when moved and a noticeable increase in size.

If you are unsure about whether your bread is ready to bake, give it a small poke with one finger and see if it springs back a bit. Too much spring means you can proof it longer; how much longer depends on the bread: let it continue to proof, checking it every 30 to 45 minutes. No spring means it has proofed too long. If this happens, don't fear. You can make modifications during the bake that accommodate an overproofed dough. For example, do not score overproofed dough—just bake it seam-side up and let it open up naturally. If your dough is so overproofed that it doesn't hold its structure anymore, it may not come out in the most uniform or pretty way, but it will still be delicious, so I always recommend baking your bread no matter what.

Here are my go-to proofing methods:

Proofing Dough: Method 1—Bowl/Banneton/Basket

If you have dough that needs help maintaining its structure, it is always good to use one of these items to proof the dough. Simply add a clean kitchen cloth, dust with whole-wheat or semolina flour, and place the dough inside it. If you plan to score the dough, place it inside the proofing vessel with the seam up so when you flip it onto your baking vessel the smooth side is facing you and ready to be scored. If you do not plan to score the bread, for a rustic look (my favorite, by the way), place the dough in the vessel with the seam down so the seam creates a natural score in the oven. After placing the dough inside the proofing vessel, cover it with a plastic bag and proof at an ambient temperature, or retard the dough in the fridge as specified in the recipe.

Proofing Dough: Method 2—Cutting Board/Couche/Kitchen Towel

If you don't have a bowl or basket available, you can proof the dough in other simple ways. If you have a baker's couche, dust it with a little flour and put your shaped dough in, seam-side down, side by side, with the couche folded up between to create layers of stability. If you don't have a couche, use a large kitchen towel in the same manner.

Alternatively, if you do not have either tool available for proofing, simply dust a cutting board with flour, semolina, or wheat bran and place your shaped dough on it. I would opt for seam-side down if using just the cutting board to keep your shape intact during the proof.

Proofing Dough: Method 3—Loaf Tin/Sheet Pan

You can use a loaf tin or sheet pan to proof many different types of doughs, even ones that will not ultimately be baked in that tin. If you have a rustic loaf that will be baked in a cast iron vessel but you want to maintain the structure of the loaf, use a loaf tin in place of an oval banneton. Simply spread a little oil in the tin before placing the dough in it.

Many of the loaves in this book, such as Choco Pan de Coco (page 99), are actually baked in a loaf tin. Some, such as the Semitas de Yema (page 117), are baked on a sheet pan.

If you are going to bake the bread in the loaf tin, proof it in the tin as well. Simply spread a little oil in the tin, put in your shaped dough, and let it proof or retard as specified in the recipe.

If you are going to bake the bread on a sheet pan, line the pan with parchment paper before placing the dough on it to proof. Make sure you leave enough space between loaves for them to rise during the proof and the bake without touching.

When proofing either in a loaf tin or on a sheet pan, create a warm environment by covering the dough with a large plastic bag that doesn't touch the dough.

Baking Bread

After the dough has proofed, it is time to bake your bread. Here are the baking methods used for the recipes in this book.

Baking Bread: Method 1—Loaf Tin

Baking bread in a loaf tin is simple. Simply pop the tin filled with proofed dough into the oven. Depending on the bread, you can score or not. This is personal preference.

Baking Bread: Method 2—Cast Iron Pots, Pans, and Dutch Ovens

This method helps create a steamy environment for the dough. Adding steam is important for certain rustic breads that need to expand during the bake and then harden to form a nice, crispy crust. The moisture from the steam helps the loaf continue to expand during the initial part of the bake, preventing the exterior from hardening too quickly. Removing steam, for example by uncovering your Dutch oven, allows the moisture to escape after your bread has risen substantially, which, in turn, begins the process of crust solidification.

It's easy to do: Simply place your cast iron vessel in the oven and preheat it to 500°F (250°C). Leave it in the oven for 30 minutes after the oven has signaled it is done preheating. This gives the iron a chance to heat to that temperature.

Using thick oven mitts or towels, remove the vessel and lightly dust it with semolina, wheat bran, or cornmeal. Flip the dough into the hot pan, score the dough, if desired, and place the lid on the pot. You can also put the dough seam-side up, meaning the side of the dough that you sealed after shaping, to give the bread a natural, rustic opening.

Put the pan back into the oven and reduce the temperature to 475°F (240°C). Note that every oven is different. For some, you may not need to lower the heat, and for others you may need to lower it further. Adjusting to an environment takes time and it will be up to you to tweak the temperatures of your oven, as needed. Bake for 15 minutes with the lid on. Remove the lid and bake for 25 minutes more so your bread gets a nice color. I usually transfer the bread out of the cast iron and onto the top oven rack for the last 10 minutes to ensure I get the dark crust I am looking for.

Baking Bread: Method 3—Sheet Pan or Pizza Stone

Believe it or not, you can achieve a nicely baked loaf of rustic bread on a sheet pan in your home oven. Similarly, a high-quality pizza stone can be used. To create steam, you will need to have another, smaller, pan in the oven, to which you will add ice.

Sheet Pan

Preheat the oven to 500°F (250°C) with the sheet pan and your smaller baking pan inside. Be aware that some sheet pans may warp at high heat.

Once the oven is preheated, using thick oven mitts or a kitchen towel, remove the sheet pan as it will not retain as much heat as cast iron or a pizza stone. Dust it liberally with semolina or cornmeal, turn the dough out on to the sheet pan and score it, as desired. If you've place the dough seam-side up, you do not need to score it. Put the sheet pan back into the oven, reduce the oven temperature to 475°F (240°C), and bake the bread as specified in the recipe.

Fill the smaller, preheated, pan with ice and put it back into the oven. As the ice melts, it will generate a steamy environment for your bread.

Pizza Stone

Preheat the oven to 500°F (250°C) with the pizza stone and a small baking pan inside. Once the oven is preheated, let it heat for an additional 30 minutes before baking your bread.

To load your bread onto the stone, you can use a cutting board dusted with flour or a pizza peel. Place the dough onto the loading vessel, score it, if desired, and load it onto the stones with a forward motion and a quick motion back.

Fill the smaller, preheated, pan with ice and put it back into the oven. As the ice melts, it will generate a steamy environment for your bread.

PART II

Recipes

Sourdough bread can be made in so many ways it can feel intimidating to start using recipes and going through the process of making this kind of bread. Remember, the reason I wrote this book is to keep things relaxed, yet creative, for you. I want you to thoroughly enjoy yourself as you progress through these recipes. I have divided the recipes into two sections to separate the rustic breads from the enriched breads.

In the rustic breads chapter (chapter 2), I include breads baked at a high heat and that have a dark, crispy crust. Although the rustic doughs may have some enriching items in them, it is not a high percentage. The overall texture, characteristics, and use of the bread also play a role in my classification as rustic. These recipes have the base ingredients of flour, water, and salt, with the occasional enriching item or two.

In the enriched breads chapter (chapter 3), I include doughs that have a larger percentage of milk, eggs, fat or oil (butter, olive oil, etc.), and some type of sugar (honey or brown sugar). These loaves are baked at a lower temperature, have a lighter crust, and, overall, are soft and delicate.

Remember, the techniques section (see page 20) covers the base methods used in many of these recipes. Instead of being redundant and explaining a shaping technique multiple times throughout the recipes, I simply cross-reference the page number for the appropriate technique. Some recipes, such as the Cinny Raisin Bagels (page 109), call for specialized shaping techniques that will be outlined within the recipe itself.

One final tip as you go through each recipe: pay attention to each levain build. Although I use the same timing for most builds, the flour types and water quantities differ. Refer to Building and Maintaining a Levain (see page 24) for a refresher, as needed.

chapter 2

RUSTIC BREADS

In this chapter I cover the types of bread I consider rustic. Although a few have a little something extra in them besides flour, water, and salt (such as the Olive Oil and Sea Salt Tin Loaf, page 49), I chose to keep them in this section as they are baked in a way that maintains the characteristics of a rustic loaf, such as a dark, crunchy exterior. These doughs make breads that can be paired with different savory options in sandwich or pizza fashion, or eaten alone dipped in oil or spread with butter or jam. You can start with the basic loaves and work your way through this chapter, or skip around straight away and bake whatever your heart desires. Besides, if you are reading this it means you have a healthy sourdough starter now and are probably excited to start using it.

PAN RUSTICO (COUNTRY BREAD)

LEVAIN BUILD

• 50 g mature sourdough starter
• 50 g bread flour
• 50 g whole-wheat flour
• 100 g warm water

FINAL DOUGH MIX

• 600 g bread flour
• 100 g whole-wheat flour
• 300 g all-purpose flour
• 730 g water
• 200 g levain
• 20 g salt
• Oil, for preparing the bowl

Rustico, or "rustic" in English, is the word I like to use to describe the baseline sourdough bread that is the starting point for understanding how to bake with a sourdough starter. Why? Because it is a process that uses just three ingredients and yields today's quintessential perception of sourdough—a crunchy, toasty, rustic loaf with a blistery dark exterior and a creamy, fluffy interior. There is something about having fresh, rustic bread in your kitchen that can't be compared with anything else. It doesn't matter what meal you are preparing to eat, fresh bread will always have a place at the table. It is the purest form of making a delicious loaf of bread. All you need to do is create a sourdough starter, understand when to use it, and grab your three ingredients.

———

To build the levain: In a tall jar or medium bowl, mix the mature starter, flours, and warm water until incorporated. Cover with a lid or clean kitchen towel and leave in a warm place for 3 to 4 hours, or until doubled in size. You can use your levain immediately, or refrigerate it for 12 hours to use later or the next day.

See Building and Maintaining a Levain (page 24) for more tips on how to tell if your levain is ready.

To make the final dough mix:

STEP 1: In a large bowl, combine the final dough ingredients as instructed using Mixing Dough: Method 1 (see page 26) until incorporated.

STEP 2: Transfer the dough to a clean bowl or tub coated with a little oil. Cover the dough and let it rest at room temperature for 30 minutes.

STEP 3: Build strength into the dough by pulling it up and folding it over in the middle of the bowl, from each side of the bowl. It is best to do this with wet hands. Cover the dough and let rest for 30 minutes more.

STEP 4: Repeat step 3. Make sure you are not tearing the dough as you pull it up and fold it over into the middle.

STEP 5: Cover the dough and let it ferment at room temperature for 4 hours.

(continued)

To shape and proof the dough:

STEP 1: Place the dough on a floured work surface, divide it in half, and shape each piece using a tension roll (see Shaping Dough: Method 1—Tension Roll, page 28).

STEP 2: Transfer the dough to proofing baskets or bowls and let sit for about 30 minutes. Cover each with a plastic bag and refrigerate overnight (8 to 12 hours). See Proofing Dough: Method 1—Bowl/Banneton/Basket (page 32) for more on this process.

To bake the bread:

You can bake these in cast iron pans, on pizza stones, or on a sheet pan. See Baking Bread: Methods 2 and 3 (pages 36 and 37) for more details:

STEP 1: Place the baking vessel in the oven and preheat to 500°F (250°C).

STEP 2: Transfer the bread to the baking vessel and bake the bread for 10 minutes. Reduce the oven temperature to 475°F (240°C) and bake the bread for 15 minutes more.

STEP 3: Let the steam out. Transfer your bread to the top rack for 20 minutes. I like to bake dark, so sometimes I go a little longer. I finish my bake with the oven door open to let out all the moisture.

STEP 4: They say to let your bread cool, but I say dig in. Warm bread with butter is the best.

❧ **TIP**: There are two ways to store bread. The first, and best, way for immediate consumption is just to leave it on your counter with a clean kitchen cloth on top. When you cut a slice, keep it cut-side down. Alternatively, let it cool completely (about 2 hours) and slice the loaf. Put your slices in a paper bag and into the freezer. When you want a slice, just toast it in a warm oven.

PAN INTEGRAL (WHOLE-WHEAT BREAD)

LEVAIN BUILD

- 50 g mature sourdough starter
- 50 g bread flour
- 50 g whole-wheat flour
- 100 g warm water

FINAL DOUGH MIX

- 800 g whole-wheat flour
- 100 g rye flour
- 100 g all-purpose flour
- 780 g water
- 210 g levain
- 20 g salt
- Oil, for preparing the bowl

In Spanish-speaking countries, *pan integral* is bread made with a significant amount of whole-wheat flour. Because there is more whole-wheat flour in this recipe, it means there will also be more water in the mix. Whole-wheat flour absorbs more liquid than white flour. Thus, the counterpart to Pan Rustico (page 43) is this flavor-packed bread that is slightly more hydrated. My favorite way to eat pan integral is by covering it in thick layers of butter and jam.

_____

To build the levain: In a tall jar or medium bowl, mix the mature starter, flours, and warm water until incorporated. Cover with a lid or clean kitchen towel and leave in a warm place for 3 to 4 hours, or until doubled in size. You can use your levain immediately, or refrigerate it for 12 hours to use later or the next day.

See Building and Maintaining a Levain (page 24) for more tips on how to tell if your levain is ready.

To make the final dough mix:

STEP 1: In a large bowl, combine the final dough ingredients as instructed using Mixing Dough: Method 1 (see page 26) until incorporated.

STEP 2: Transfer the dough to a clean bowl or tub coated with a little oil. Cover the dough with a clean kitchen towel and let rest at room temperature for 30 minutes.

STEP 3: Build strength into the dough by pulling it up and folding it over in the middle of the bowl, from each side of the bowl. It is best to do this with wet hands. Cover the dough and let rest for 30 minutes more.

STEP 4: Repeat step 3 two more times. You need to build more strength into a dough made with a significant amount of whole-wheat flour, such as this one. Make sure you are not tearing the dough as you pull it up and fold it over into the middle.

STEP 5: Cover the dough and let it ferment at room temperature for 4 hours.

(continued)

To shape and proof the dough:

STEP 1: Place the dough on a floured work surface, divide it in half, and shape each piece using a tension roll (see Shaping Dough: Method 1—Tension Roll, page 28).

STEP 2: Transfer the dough to proofing baskets or bowls and let sit for about 30 minutes. Cover each with a plastic bag and refrigerate overnight (8 to 12 hours). See Proofing Dough: Method 1—Bowl/Banneton/Basket (page 32) for more on this process.

To bake the bread:

STEP 1: Place your baking vessel in the oven and preheat to 500°F (250°C).

STEP 2: Transfer the bread to the baking vessel and bake the bread for 10 minutes. Reduce the oven temperature to 475°F (240°C) and bake the bread for 15 minutes more.

STEP 3: Let the steam out. Transfer your bread to the top rack for 20 minutes. I like to bake dark, so sometimes I go a little longer. I finish my bake with the oven door open to let out all the moisture.

STEP 4: Definitely let this whole-wheat bread cool for 20 minutes to ensure the inside cooks thoroughly.

OLIVE OIL AND
SEA SALT TIN LOAF

YIELD: 2 LOAVES

LEVAIN BUILD

- 100 g mature sourdough starter
- 200 g bread flour
- 180 g warm water

FINAL DOUGH MIX

- 1 kg all-purpose flour
- 200 g olive oil, plus more for coating
- 650 g water
- 25 g sea salt, plus more for sprinkling
- 350 g levain
- Oil, for proofing and baking

One of the most simple yet satisfying types of bread is a sandwich loaf baked in a tin. This versatile bread delivers the perfect slice—be it thick or thin—because of its soft, tender, moist interior and crackling light brown crust. When I started making sourdough bread, it was not long before I began to experiment with loaves that had a different look and consistency than the traditional rustic-style breads. Olive oil is one of the best oils to use to add moisture on the inside and a crackling texture to the crust. Because of the olive oil and sea salt sprinkled on top, each slice is the perfect bite of bread. Most people don't associate a soft, fluffy loaf for slicing with the word *sourdough*, but once you taste the flavor of the fermentation there is no mistaking that this is another naturally leavened beauty.

———

To build the levain: In a tall jar or medium bowl, mix the mature starter, flour, and warm water until incorporated. Cover with a lid or clean kitchen towel and leave in a warm place for 3 to 4 hours, or until doubled in size. You can use your levain immediately, or refrigerate it for 12 hours to use later or the next day.

See Building and Maintaining a Levain (page 24) for more tips on how to tell if your levain is ready.

To make the final dough mix:

STEP 1: In a large bowl, mix all the final dough ingredients until there is no dry flour remaining. Once the ingredients are just combined, turn the dough out on to your work surface and knead it with your palm, as described in Mixing Dough: Method 2 (page 27), until it is smooth on the surface.

STEP 2: Transfer the dough to a large, clean bowl coated with a little oil and let rise at room temperature for 4 hours. You do not need to stretch or fold this dough during the initial rise. Cover the dough and refrigerate it, without shaping, for 8 hours.

To shape and proof the dough:

STEP 1: Lightly coat 2 loaf tins with olive oil. Set aside.

STEP 2: Take the dough out of the fridge. Place the dough on a lightly floured work surface, divide it in half, and shape each piece using a tension roll (see Shaping Dough: Method 1—Tension Roll, page 28). Put each loaf into a prepared tin.

STEP 3: Cover the dough and let proof for 3 to 4 hours, or until soft to the touch and jiggly when you move the pan.

To bake the bread:

STEP 1: Preheat the oven to 450°F (230°C).

STEP 2: Rub some olive oil onto the surface of the loaves and drizzle each with a sprinkle of sea salt. No need to score these loaves.

STEP 3: Bake your loaves for 30 minutes, or until golden brown on top. Let them cool completely if you want to slice the bread for sandwich use.

COCO RUGBRØD

My other pan de coco recipe (see Choco Pan de Coco, page 99) is a refreshing take on this traditional Honduran bread because it's much lighter and a tad sweeter than its native counterpart. The classic version found in barrios and on dinner tables next to a bowl of hot *sopa de caracol*, or with a morning coffee, is typically a dense bread made with harina integral, or whole-wheat flour. But it wasn't until I was eating a classic Danish rye bread, rugbrød, that I had the idea of taking yet another stab at pan de coco. Rugbrød is both delicious and interesting because of how many different textures are involved. And, because it doesn't use white flour, it is packed with more nutritious flavor. So, this time around, I want to explore the density of a more authentic bread you might find in Honduras but also incorporate different textures into the bread, similar to a rugbrød.

50

NEW WORLD SOURDOUGH

LEVAIN BUILD

- 60 g mature sourdough starter
- 100 g bread flour
- 20 g whole-wheat flour
- 100 g warm water

FINAL DOUGH MIX

- 200 g coconut milk
- 100 g water
- 200 g levain
- 250 g whole-wheat flour
- 200 g all-purpose flour
- 25 g oat flour
- 25 g rye flour
- 50 g sunflower seeds
- 28 g light brown sugar
- 28 g coconut oil, plus more for preparing the loaf tins and coating the loaves
- 10 g salt
- 200 g shredded coconut
- 150 g quinoa

To build the levain: In a tall jar or medium bowl, mix the mature starter, flours, and warm water until incorporated. Cover with a lid or clean kitchen towel and leave in a warm place for 3 to 4 hours, or until doubled in size. You can use your levain immediately, or refrigerate it for 12 hours to use later or the next day.

See Building and Maintaining a Levain (page 24) for more tips on how to tell if your levain is ready.

To make the final dough mix:

STEP 1: In a small microwave-safe bowl or a saucepan, combine the coconut milk and water. Warm slightly in the microwave (or on the stovetop in a small pan). Make sure the mixture isn't boiling or too hot to the touch. Transfer to a large bowl.

STEP 2: Add the levain and dissolve it in the warm coconut water mixture.

STEP 3: Using your hands, mix in the flours, sunflower seeds, brown sugar, coconut oil, salt, shredded coconut, and quinoa as instructed in Mixing Dough: Method 2 (page 27) until incorporated.

STEP 4: Turn the dough out on to a work surface and knead it with your palm until smooth.

STEP 5: Transfer the dough to a clean, large bowl and let ferment for 5 or 6 hours. Cover the dough and refrigerate it to ferment in a cold environment for up to 12 hours.

To shape and proof the dough:

STEP 1: Lightly coat a loaf tin with coconut oil. Set aside.

STEP 2: Turn the dough out on to a floured work surface and shape the dough into a log using a tension roll (see Shaping Dough: Method 1—Tension Roll, page 28). Place the log horizontally into the prepared loaf tin. Let the dough proof for 3 to 4 hours until spongy and soft to the touch, but not sticky.

To bake the bread:

STEP 1: Thirty minutes before the proof is complete, preheat the oven to 375°F (190°C).

STEP 2: Baste the loaf with coconut oil and top with the coconut and quinoa.

STEP 3: Bake for 40 minutes, or until golden brown. You may need to rotate your pan halfway through the baking time. Some ovens have hotspots to watch for and you will learn over time as you bake how evenly your oven bakes things. Hot spots are typically at the back corners of the oven, so if these begin to get dark before other parts of the bread, you should rotate the loaf to get an even color. This bread is BEST when eaten hot out of the oven.

❧ **TIP**: This loaf is best eaten sliced with delicious toppings, such as avocado, pickled onions, or fresh cheeses.

TOASTY SEED SOUR

SEED MIX

- 30 g sesame seeds
- 20 g flaxseed
- 20 g sunflower seeds
- 10 g pumpkin seeds
- 10 g old-fashioned rolled oats
- 210 g water

LEVAIN BUILD

- 50 g mature sourdough starter
- 50 g bread flour
- 50 g whole-wheat flour
- 100 g warm water

FINAL DOUGH MIX

- 600 g bread flour
- 300 g whole-wheat flour
- 100 g all-purpose flour
- 700 g water, divided
- 200 g levain
- 20 g salt

I remember the day I preheated my oven without realizing I had left a sheet pan full of raw seeds inside. As I was preparing to bake a different loaf, I was struck with a toasty, nutty, earthy aroma that made me feel as if I was deep in the forest camping. Once I realized I had accidentally toasted some seeds, I knew I needed to use them. I let them cool, soaked them, and used the soaking water directly in the dough mix. Because of the flavor of these crispy seeds, this was one of the best baking accidents I ever made. Note: Before you start mixing, you will toast seeds and let them soak overnight.

———

To build the levain: In a tall jar or medium bowl, mix the mature starter, flours, and warm water until incorporated. Cover with a lid or clean kitchen towel and leave in a warm place for 3 to 4 hours, or until doubled in size. You can use your levain immediately, or refrigerate it for 12 hours to use later or the next day.

See Building and Maintaining a Levain (page 24) for more tips on how to tell if your levain is ready.

To make the seed mix:

STEP 1: Preheat the oven to 350°F (180°C).

STEP 2: On a sheet pan, combine the seeds and oats. Toast for 5 to 10 minutes until all seeds are dark brown/black. Let cool completely. Transfer to a small bowl and stir in the water. Cover and refrigerate overnight.

To make the final dough mix:

STEP 1: The next day, in a large bowl, mix the flours and 650 g of water until there is no dry flour remaining. Let sit for 30 minutes.

STEP 2: Add the levain, the water from the soaked seeds, and the salt. Squeeze the water and levain into the dough until incorporated. Let rest for 30 minutes more.

STEP 3: Add the seeds and the remaining 50 g of water if the dough is not too wet. Your seeds may or may not absorb a lot of water, so add what makes you comfortable.

STEP 4: Complete a total of two stretch and folds every 30 minutes.

STEP 5: Cover the dough and let it ferment at room temperature for 4 hours.

(continued on page 56)

To shape and proof the dough:

STEP 1: Place the dough on a floured work surface, divide it in half, and shape each piece using the rounding technique (see Shaping Dough: Method 2—Rounding, page 28).

STEP 2: Transfer the dough to proofing baskets or bowls and let proof for about 30 minutes. Cover each with a plastic bag and refrigerate overnight (8 to 12 hours). See Proofing Dough: Method 1—Bowl/Banneton/Basket (page 32) for more on this process.

To bake the bread:

You can bake these loaves in cast iron pans, on pizza stones, or even on a sheet pan. See Baking Bread: Methods 2 and 3 (pages 36 and 37) for more guidance.

STEP 1: Place the baking vessels in the oven and preheat to 500°F (250°C).

STEP 2: Transfer the bread to the baking vessel and bake the bread for 10 minutes. Reduce the oven temperature to 475°F (240°C) and bake the bread for 15 minutes more.

STEP 3: Let the steam out. Transfer the bread to the top rack for 20 minutes. I like to bake dark, so sometimes I go a little longer. I finish my bake with the oven door open to let out all the moisture.

STEP 4: The flavor of this bread is best enjoyed alone at first, so you can get the full toasty seed flavor. It also makes fantastic sandwich bread!

PAN GALLEGO (BREAD OF GALICIA)

LEVAIN BUILD

- 50 g mature sourdough starter
- 50 g bread flour
- 25 g rye flour
- 25 g whole-wheat flour
- 90 g warm water

FINAL DOUGH MIX

- 800 g water, divided
- 850 g bread flour
- 150 g rye flour
- 200 g levain
- 20 g salt

Bread from every Spanish-speaking country intrigues me, so I knew I had to investigate the various bread-making techniques from Spain. I came across photos of *pan Gallego*, or Galician bread, and had never seen anything like it. The rustic shape and nature of it do not call for a score before baking, which is always a plus for me. With a dark, caramelized crust and a very distinct knot tied on the top of the loaf, this was worth researching. Although I don't have access to the flour that is native to Galicia, Spain, I spoke with bakers in the area who recommended using a strong white flour and rye. They also told me that the magic of pan Gallego is all in the knot! You want enough rye flour to give the crumb a distinct speckle, but enough strength to be able to knot the dough before baking.

To build the levain: In a tall jar or medium bowl, mix the mature starter, flours, and warm water until incorporated. Cover with a lid or clean kitchen towel and leave in a warm place for 3 to 4 hours, or until doubled in size. You can use your levain immediately, or refrigerate it for 12 hours to use later or the next day.

See Building and Maintaining a Levain (page 24) for more tips on how to tell if your levain is ready.

To make the final dough mix:

This dough is a bit more hydrated than most others in this book. The key to hand mixing highly hydrated dough is to add the water as slowly as possible.

STEP 1: Place 650 g of the water into a large bowl. Add the flours and mix.

STEP 2: Add 50 g of water and combine as instructed using Mixing Dough: Method 1 (page 26) until incorporated. Let the dough relax for 30 minutes.

STEP 3: Add the levain and 50 g of water and mix to dissolve the levain. Let rest for 1 hour.

STEP 4: Add the salt and the remaining 50 g of water. Squeeze the salt and water into the dough until incorporated and you have a smooth surface.

STEP 5: Complete total of two stretch and folds every 30 minutes.

STEP 6: Let the dough rise for 4 hours. When this initial fermentation is complete, you will notice a smooth, bubbly surface. Cover the dough and refrigerate it for 8 to 10 hours.

(continued)

To shape and proof the dough:

STEP 1: Place the dough on a floured work surface, divide it in half, and shape each piece using the rounding technique (see Shaping Dough: Method 2—Rounding, page 28).

STEP 2: Transfer the dough to proofing baskets or bowls. Cover with a plastic bag or kitchen cloth and let proof for 3 hours.

To bake the bread:

Refer to Baking Bread: Method 2—Cast Iron Pots, Pans, and Dutch Ovens (page 36).

STEP 1: Place your baking vessel in the oven and preheat to 500°F (250°C).

STEP 2: Turn the dough out on to a floured work surface, seam-side down. It's time to make the signature knot. Grab the very top of the dough with your fingers and, pinching it, pull it up as high as you can. With your other hand, tie this elongated dough into a knot and let it settle back down. Repeat with the other dough piece.

STEP 3: Transfer the dough to the baking vessel and bake for 10 minutes. Reduce the oven temperature to 475°F (240°C) and bake the bread for 15 minutes more until you have a dark, blistery crust.

❧ **TIP**: This loaf goes extremely well with a nice, warm soup. Pull it apart and dip it in to enjoy.

BIROTE

LEVAIN BUILD

- 50 g mature sourdough starter
- 100 g bread flour
- 90 g warm water

FINAL DOUGH MIX

- 400 g all-purpose flour
- 100 g bread flour
- 315 g water
- 100 g levain
- 50 g light beer, divided
- Juice of 1 lime
- 10 g salt

I find nothing more satisfying than recreating the unique breads of Latin America in my very own kitchen. I especially love when the bread is meant to be stuffed with savory fillings and drowned in spicy salsa—in Mexico, the *torta ahogada* is just that. Birote (pronounced bee-row-teh) is a crunchy, darkly baked sourdough bread said to have a flavor unique to the environment of Guadalajara, but if you grab your favorite beer and some limes, you'll come pretty close!

———

To build the levain: In a tall jar or medium bowl, mix the mature starter, flour, and warm water until incorporated. Cover with a lid or clean kitchen towel and leave in a warm place for 3 to 4 hours, or until doubled in size. You can use your levain immediately, or refrigerate it for 12 hours to use at a later time or the next day.

See Building and Maintaining a Levain (page 24) for more tips on how to tell if your levain is ready.

To make the final dough mix:

STEP 1: In a large bowl, mix the flours and water. Let this mixture rest for 30 minutes.

STEP 2: Add the levain, the beer, and the lime juice. Using your fingers, squeeze together and incorporate the ingredients until the dough is smooth and no excess liquid remains. Cover the dough with a cloth and let rest for 30 minutes.

STEP 3: Stretch the dough into itself a few times and flip it over in the bowl. Let rest for 30 minutes.

STEP 4: Repeat the stretching. Let the dough ferment at room temperature for 3½ hours.

STEP 5: Cover the dough and refrigerate overnight, 8 to 12 hours.

To shape and proof the dough:

STEP 1: Place the dough on a floured work surface, divide it into 5 pieces (roughly 200 g each), and shape each piece with a tension roll (see Shaping Dough: Method 1—Tension Roll, page 28).

STEP 2: Transfer the dough to a cutting board, couche, or kitchen cloth. See Proofing Dough: Method 2—Cutting Board/Couche/ Kitchen Towel Proof (page 32) for more on this process. Let proof for 1 to 2 hours (see Proofing Dough, page 32, for more on how to tell when your dough is ready to bake).

To bake the bread:

I prefer to bake these on a sheet pan dusted with semolina. See Baking Bread: Methods 2 and 3 (pages 36 and 37) for more guidance here.

STEP 1: Place the baking vessel in the oven and preheat to 500°F (250°C).

STEP 2: Transfer the bread to the baking vessel and bake for 10 minutes. Reduce the oven temperature to 475°F (240°C) and bake the bread for 15 minutes more.

STEP 3: Let the steam out. Transfer the bread to the top rack for 5 to 10 minutes, or until it is dark brown—keep an eye on it. Remember, you want a dark bread with a thick crust so you can create a delicious soaked sandwich. Don't be afraid to bake it longer than you are used to.

STEP 4: Let your bread cool and enjoy it as a soaked sandwich, like the *torta ahogada*, or with oil, vinegar, butter, or jam.

"I FIND
NOTHING MORE
SATISFYING THAN
RECREATING
THE UNIQUE
BREADS OF
LATIN AMERICA
IN MY VERY OWN
KITCHEN."

PAN DE AGUA
(WATER BREAD)

LEVAIN BUILD

- 50 g mature sourdough starter
- 100 g bread flour
- 100 g warm water

FINAL DOUGH MIX

- 500 g bread flour
- 500 g all-purpose flour
- 660 g water, divided
- 75 g granulated sugar
- 185 g levain
- 20 g salt
- Semolina, or cornmeal, for dusting
- 2 egg whites
- Boiling water, for baking

The island of Puerto Rico is home to a unique style of cooking found at every corner, and some of the bread I had there inspired me to make variations at home. One of my favorite meals was a tripleta sandwich from a street corner vendor. After devouring the sandwich, I asked about the bread and whether it was made locally. "Of course!" he said. With great pride, he graciously took the time to describe the unique method of baking pan de agua. The crisp, light, and moist bread is put into a cold oven with pans of boiling water and baked as the oven comes to temperature. He explained that this method helps create the texture of the bread, and I had no choice but to start figuring out how to make my own.

———

To build the levain: In a tall jar or medium bowl, mix the mature starter, flour, and warm water until incorporated. Cover with a lid or clean kitchen towel and leave in a warm place for 3 to 4 hours, or until doubled in size. You can use your levain immediately, or refrigerate it for 12 hours to use later or the next day.

See Building and Maintaining a Levain (page 24) for more tips on how to tell if your levain is ready.

To make the final dough mix:

STEP 1: In a large bowl, mix the flours, 650 g of water, the granulated sugar, levain, and salt as instructed using Mixing Dough: Method 2 (page 27) until incorporated.

STEP 2: Let your mixture ferment at room temperature for 4 hours. Cover the dough and refrigerate for 12 hours.

To shape and proof the dough:

STEP 1: Place the dough on a liberally floured work surface, divide it into 400-g pieces (about 5), and let rest at room temperature for 30 minutes.

STEP 2: Shape each dough piece using a tension roll (see Shaping Dough: Method 1— Tension Roll, page 28).

STEP 3: Dust a sheet pan with semolina or cornmeal and put your shaped loaves on the prepared pan to proof for 3 hours (see Proofing Dough, page 32, for more on this process).

To bake the bread:

STEP 1: In a small bowl, whisk the egg whites and remaining 10 g of water. Brush the loaves with the egg white mixture.

STEP 2: Place the sheet pan with the loaves on it and an empty sheet pan into a cold oven. Pour the boiling water (about 200 g) into the empty sheet pan.

STEP 3: Preheat the oven to 375°F (190°C).

STEP 4: Bake the bread for 20 minutes until you have a nice, shiny, light golden brown crust, depending on your egg white mixture consistency. You will notice a crackling texture as well.

PLANTAIN SOURDOUGH

LEVAIN BUILD

- 60 g mature sourdough starter
- 60 g bread flour
- 60 g whole-wheat flour
- 100 g warm water

FINAL DOUGH MIX

- 700 g bread flour
- 300 g whole-wheat flour
- 700 g water
- 200 g levain
- 200 g uncooked quinoa
- 3 plantains, peeled
- 30 g honey
- 20 g salt

When I first moved to Miami I began selling my own bread at the local farmer's market. I decided I wanted to make something that was naturally leavened and incorporated ingredients that were abundant and with which I was familiar. *Platanos* are a huge part of my culinary culture, and the idea for this recipe dawned on me one day while walking by a bunch of *platanos maduros* (ripe plantains). I bought a handful and got to work figuring out how to make a delicious, rustic loaf of bread that incorporated their mildly sweet flavor. After a few tries, I wanted more texture so I added the quinoa, and since then I've never looked back. This loaf is amazing for breakfast, so load up your plate with black beans, cheese, eggs, and some thick slices of plantain sourdough!

To build the levain: In a tall jar or medium bowl, mix the mature starter, flours, and warm water until incorporated. Cover with a lid or clean kitchen towel and leave in a warm place for 3 to 4 hours, or until doubled in size. You can use your levain immediately, or refrigerate it for 12 hours to use later or the next day.

See Building and Maintaining a Levain (page 24) for more tips on how to tell if your levain is ready.

To make the final dough mix:

STEP 1: In a large bowl, mix the flours, water, and levain as instructed using Mixing Dough: Method 1 (page 26) until incorporated.

STEP 2: Add the quinoa and squeeze the dough until it is evenly incorporated. Let the dough rest for 30 minutes.

STEP 3: While the dough rests, in a medium saucepan over high heat, combine the plantains and enough water to cover. Bring to a boil and cook until they are completely soft, about 15 minutes, and you can poke them a knife or fork without any resistance. Drain the water and mash the plantains into the consistency of mashed potatoes. Cool the plantains completely by placing them in the freezer, but do not let them begin freezing.

STEP 4: Once the plantains are cool, add a splash of water and half the mashed plantains to the dough. Stretch the dough and fold it into the middle a few times. Rotating your bowl will help you stretch each side. Flip the dough over. Add the remaining plantains on top and gently stretch and fold the dough again. Let the dough rest for 30 minutes more and repeat the stretching process.

STEP 5: Let the dough ferment at room temperature for 4 hours.

(continued)

To shape and proof the dough:

STEP 1: Place the dough on a floured work surface, divide it in half, and shape each piece using a tension roll (see Shaping Dough: Method 1—Tension Roll, page 28).

STEP 2: Proof following the Proofing Dough: Method 1—Bowl/Banneton/Basket (page 32). Cover the loaves and refrigerate overnight, or 12 hours.

To bake the bread:

Bake the bread following Baking Bread: Method 2—Cast Iron Pots, Pans, and Dutch Ovens (page 36).

STEP 1: Place your cast iron vessel into the oven and preheat to 500°F (250°C).

STEP 2: Transfer the bread to the baking vessel and bake for 10 minutes. Reduce the oven temperature to 475°F (240°C) and bake the bread for 15 minutes more.

STEP 3: Let the steam out. Transfer the bread to the top rack for 5 to 10 minutes more. Enjoy!

RUSTIC OLIVE AND PARMESAN BREAD

LEVAIN BUILD

- 50 g mature sourdough starter
- 50 g bread flour
- 50 g whole-wheat flour
- 100 g warm water

FINAL DOUGH MIX

- 600 g bread flour
- 200 g all-purpose flour
- 200 g whole-wheat flour
- 720 g water
- 210 g levain
- 20 g salt
- 200 g Kalamata olives, pitted and halved
- 50 g shredded Parmesan cheese
- Oil, for coating

I was once told by someone that olive bread should just be olive bread. Although I loved the saying, I completely disregarded the advice, as evidenced by one of my favorite recipes you'll find in chapter 3, Muffaletta Rolls (page 135). However, the simplicity of olive flavor does need to be respected, so I decided to make a nice rustic loaf that highlights the delicious flavor of the olive, and goes great on your dinner table or for sandwich use. I needed, however, to add a different texture to the bread, so I topped it with loads of Parmesan cheese mid-bake for a nice crunchy, salty bite that accompanies the wonderful overload of olive flavor. I suggest you get some balsamic vinegar and some good cheese to enjoy slices of this fresh, beautiful bread.

To build the levain: In a tall jar or medium bowl, mix the mature starter, flours, and warm water until incorporated. Cover with a lid or clean kitchen towel and leave in a warm place for 3 to 4 hours, or until doubled in size. You can use your levain immediately, or refrigerate it for 12 hours to use later or the next day.

See Building and Maintaining a Levain (page 24) for more tips on how to tell if your levain is ready.

To make the final dough mix:

STEP 1: In a large bowl, mix the flours, water, levain, and salt as instructed using the Mixing Dough: Method 1 (page 26).

STEP 2: Coat a clean bowl or tub with a little bit of oil and transfer the dough to it. Cover the dough and let rest at room temperature for 30 minutes.

STEP 3: Spread half the olives on top of the dough, then stretch and fold the dough over into the middle, from each side. It is best to do this with wet hands. Cover the dough and let rest for 30 minutes more.

STEP 4: Spread the remaining olives over the dough. Repeat the stretching and folding. Make sure you are not tearing the dough as you pull it up and fold it over into the middle.

STEP 5: Cover the dough and let it ferment at room temperature for 4 hours.

To shape and proof the dough:

STEP 1: Place the dough on a floured work surface, divide it in half, and shape each piece with a tension roll (see Shaping Dough: Method 1—Tension Roll, page 28).

STEP 2: Transfer the dough to proofing baskets or bowls and let proof for about 30 minutes. Cover the dough with a plastic bag and refrigerate it overnight, 8 to 12 hours). See Proofing Dough (page 32), for more on this process.

(continued)

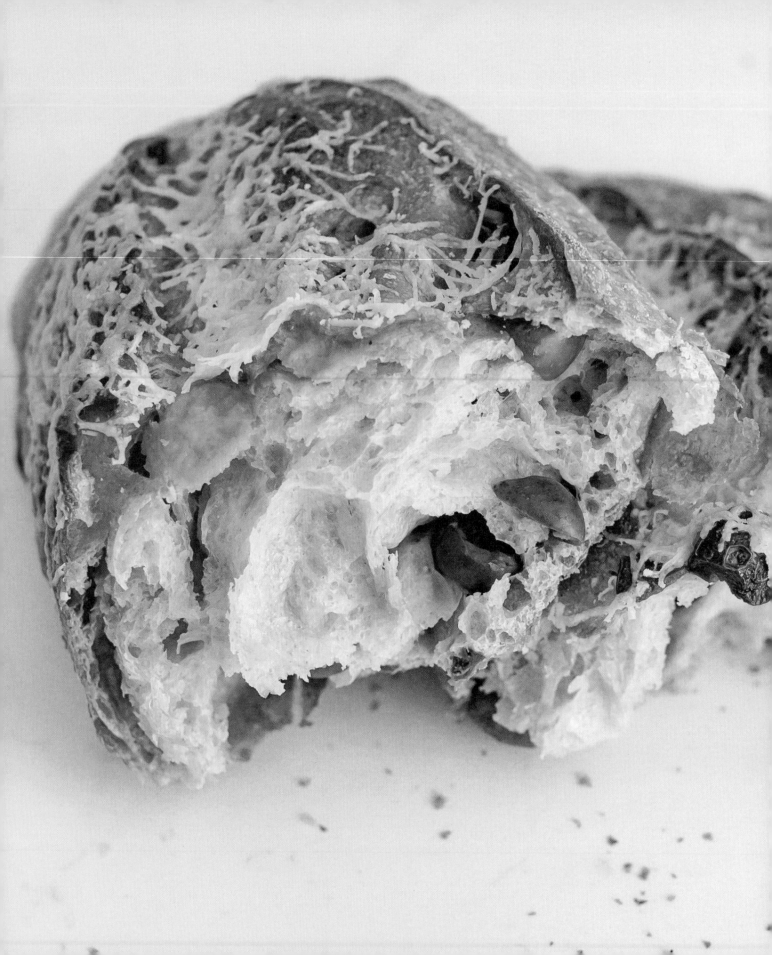

To bake the bread:

Bake the bread following Baking Bread: Method 2—Cast Iron Pots, Pans, and Dutch Ovens (page 36).

STEP 1: Place a cast iron vessel into the oven and preheat to 500°F (250°C).

STEP 2: Bake the bread for 10 minutes. Reduce the oven temperature to 475°F (240°C) and bake the bread for 15 minutes more.

STEP 3: Let the steam out by uncovering the dough.

STEP 4: Sprinkle the Parmesan cheese on top of the dough and transfer the bread to the top rack for 20 minutes. I like to bake dark, so sometimes I go a little longer. I finish my bake with the oven door open to let all the moisture out.

STEP 5: Let this loaf cool for 30 minutes, slice it, and enjoy!

CIABATTA

LEVAIN BUILD

- 50 g mature sourdough starter
- 100 g bread flour
- 100 g warm water

FINAL DOUGH MIX

- 200 g bread flour
- 800 g all-purpose flour
- 700 g water
- 100 g levain
- 20 g salt
- Olive oil, for coating

Ciabatta is a very forgiving and naturally beautiful bread. The irregular shape makes each loaf unique. The outside crust is a maze of natural crackling indentations that look like the flow of little rivers. As you cut your ciabatta in half, you'll notice crunchy shards of crust falling off as you start to see the creamy, fluffy interior. Making a good ciabatta does not require much effort, especially if you keep an open mind and accept the freestyle nature of this process. The dough does not need to be messed with much—it is proofed in flour and baked with no score. My only requirement is to bake these loaves nice and dark for a great crunch and flavor. The good thing about this dough is you can make your ciabatta in any size that suits your need—whether for sandwiches, table bread, or simply eaten alone.

To build the levain: In a tall jar or medium bowl, mix the mature starter, flour, and warm water until incorporated. Cover with a lid or clean kitchen towel and leave in a warm place for 3 to 4 hours, or until doubled in size. You can use your levain immediately, or refrigerate it for 12 hours to use later or the next day.

See Building and Maintaining a Levain (page 24) for more tips on how to tell if your levain is ready.

To make the final dough mix:

STEP 1: In a large bowl, mix the flours, water, levain, and salt as instructed using Mixing Dough: Method 1 (page 26) until incorporated.

STEP 2: Coat another large bowl or bin with olive oil and transfer the dough to it. Cover the dough and let sit at room temperature overnight, up to 12 hours.

To shape and proof the dough:

STEP 1: Dump out the dough and divide it with your hands into 3 or 4 rectangles. They aren't going to be perfect.

STEP 2: Dust a sheet pan heavily with flour and put your ciabatta loaves on it. Cover the loaves and let proof at room temperature for 3 to 4 hours, or until they have grown and are springy to the touch.

To bake the bread:

Bake the bread following Baking Bread: Method 2—Cast Iron Pots, Pans, and Dutch Ovens (page 36).

STEP 1: Place your cast iron vessel into the oven and preheat to 500°F (250°C).

STEP 2: Transfer the bread to the baking vessel and bake for 10 minutes. Reduce the oven temperature to 475°F (240°C) and bake the bread for 15 minutes more.

STEP 3: Let the steam out. Transfer the bread to the top rack for 5 to 10 minutes more.

ENGLISH MUFFINS

LEVAIN BUILD

- 50 g mature sourdough starter
- 50 g bread flour
- 50 g whole-wheat flour
- 100 g warm water

FINAL DOUGH MIX

- 250 g bread flour
- 100 g all-purpose flour
- 50 g semolina flour, plus more for dusting
- 50 g whole-wheat flour
- 50 g spelt flour
- 310 g water
- 100 g levain
- 20 g salt
- Cornmeal, for dusting

My mom went through a phase of always having store-bought English muffins in the fridge. She would eat them plain, or for breakfast as a sandwich. To be quite honest, I was not fond of these at all and, naturally, this sparked the curiosity in me to figure out a way to create an enjoyable English muffin. The priority is to be able to create the nooks and crannies that make them a perfect vessel for sweet and savory spreads. Second to getting the texture right is flavor. I want the comforting flavor of an English muffin with a touch of whole grains and strong hints of proper fermentation. When they don't taste like they've been sitting in a plastic bag for a long time, English muffins are actually quite phenomenal. A must-make item for any home that needs quick and delicious breakfast bread.

—————

To build the levain: In a tall jar or medium bowl, mix the mature starter, flours, and warm water until incorporated. Cover with a lid or clean kitchen towel and leave in a warm place for 3 to 4 hours, or until doubled in size. You can use your levain immediately, or refrigerate it for 12 hours to use later or the next day.

See Building and Maintaining a Levain (page 24) for more tips on how to tell if your levain is ready.

To make the final dough mix:

STEP 1: In a large bowl, mix the flours, water, levain, and salt as instructed using Mixing Dough: Method 2 (page 27) until incorporated.

STEP 2: Cover the dough and let ferment at room temperature for 6 hours. Refrigerate the dough for 15 hours more.

To shape and proof the dough:

STEP 1: Turn the dough out on to a floured work surface and stretch the dough into a rectangle about ½ inch (1 cm) thick.

STEP 2: Line a sheet pan with parchment paper and dust it liberally with semolina and cornmeal.

STEP 3: Using about a 3- or 4-inch (7.5 or 10 cm) round baking ring or a cup, cut out about 10 circles from the dough. Place each dough circle on the prepared baking sheet. Dust the tops with a bit more cornmeal.

STEP 4: Cover the English muffins and let proof at room temperature for 1 hour.

To cook the muffins:

STEP 1: Heat a cast iron skillet over medium-low heat.

STEP 2: Dust the skillet with cornmeal and semolina.

STEP 3: Place the muffins in the skillet and cook for 4 to 5 minutes per side until golden brown on the top and bottom and lighter on the sides, with darker bits of cornmeal or semolina on top. The time may vary depending on your stove.

STEP 4: Let rest for about 20 minutes to ensure the inside is fully cooked before cutting.

PRETZEL BUNS

LEVAIN BUILD

- 50 g mature sourdough starter
- 100 g bread flour
- 100 g warm water

FINAL DOUGH MIX

- 400 g bread flour
- 100 g all-purpose flour
- 290 g water
- 30 g unsalted butter
- 20 g granulated sugar
- 2 g diastatic malt powder
- 100 g levain
- 10 g salt
- Olive oil, for dabbing

POACHING

- 1 kg water
- 30 g baking soda

After spending time in Germany, I was a man on a mission. The number of pretzels I ate was unreal—they were just so insanely delicious and addictive, I couldn't help myself. Nothing beats the aromas of good beer, quality meats, and pretzels; the experience lingered in my mind for some time. I knew I needed a dough that wasn't too hydrated, with a good chew and a soft interior. Although, typically, these are poached in a lye solution, I don't opt to keep this around my house. In this recipe, you'll use baking soda for your alkaline poaching solution and get a great result.

———

To build the levain: In a tall jar or bowl, mix the mature starter, flour, and warm water until incorporated. Cover with a lid or clean kitchen towel and leave in a warm place for 3 to 4 hours, or until doubled in size. You can use your levain immediately, or refrigerate it for 12 hours to use later or the next day.

See Building and Maintaining a Levain (page 24) for more tips on how to tell if your levain is ready.

To make the final dough mix:

STEP 1: In a large bowl, mix all the final dough mix ingredients as instructed using Mixing Dough: Method 2 (page 26) until incorporated.

STEP 2: Cover the dough and let ferment at room temperature for 4 hours.

To shape and proof the dough:

STEP 1: Line 2 baking sheets with parchment paper and set aside.

STEP 2: Turn the dough out on a work surface and divide it into 55-g pieces (about 15) and shape each piece using the balling up technique (see Shaping Dough: Method 3—Balling Up, page 31). Place the dough balls on the prepared sheet pans in rows of 2 by 6.

STEP 3: Dab each bun with olive oil and wrap the pans with plastic wrap. Let the dough sit at room temperature for 20 minutes. Refrigerate the sheet pans overnight, for 15 hours, for cold fermentation.

To poach and bake the buns:

STEP 1: Preheat the oven to 375°F (190°C).

STEP 2: In a large pot over high heat, combine the water and baking soda and bring to a boil. As soon as there is a rolling boil, turn the heat down to maintain a simmer.

STEP 3: Add your rolls, 2 at a time, and poach for 45 seconds per side. I usually use a metal strainer, spider, or pasta scoop for this. Transfer the poached rolls back to the sheet pan. Repeat with the remaining rolls.

STEP 4: Use a serrated knife, cut a small X in each roll. Bake for 25 minutes, or until they are a nice dark brown color.

STEP 5: Let your buns cool for 20 minutes and enjoy!

NEW ORLEANS FRENCH BREAD

LEVAIN BUILD

- 50 g mature sourdough starter
- 100 g bread flour
- 60 g warm water

FINAL DOUGH MIX

- 500 g bread flour
- 300 g water
- 50 g shortening, or vegetable oil
- 25 g granulated sugar
- 100 g levain
- 10 g salt
- Semolina, for dusting

There is nothing quite like a loaf of good ol' New Orleans–style French bread. My favorite part of going to the supermarket growing up was picking up a loaf of French bread. In New Orleans, it is a long crisp loaf that is perfect for po' boy sandwiches. A light brown crust that shatters, a soft but chewy interior, and a subtle flavor that doesn't overpower your sandwich. Locals will tell you, if the bread isn't right, then the sandwich isn't right. I agree, and I think you can make French bread at home just as delicious as what you can find at your favorite po' boy shop.

———

To build the levain: In a tall jar or medium bowl, mix the mature starter, flour, and warm water until incorporated. Cover with a lid or clean kitchen towel and leave in a warm place for 3 to 4 hours, or until doubled in size. You can use your levain immediately, or refrigerate it for 12 hours to use later or the next day.

See Building and Maintaining a Levain (page 24) for more tips on how to tell if your levain is ready.

To make the final dough mix:

STEP 1: In a large bowl, mix all the final dough mix ingredients as instructed using Mixing Dough: Method 2 (page 27) until no dry flour remains.

STEP 2: Cover the dough with a damp cloth and let ferment at room temperature for 4 hours. Refrigerate the dough, covered, for 12 hours more.

To shape and proof the dough:

STEP 1: Turn the dough out on to a work surface. Divide it in half and shape each piece using a tension roll (see Shaping Dough: Method 1—Tension Roll, page 28).

STEP 2: Dust a sheet pan with semolina and place your shaped loaves on it. Using a pastry brush, brush the loaves with water. Cover the loaves with a damp cloth and let proof at room temperature for 3 hours.

To bake the bread:

There is no need to score these loaves.

STEP 1: Preheat the oven to 375°F (190°C).

STEP 2: Bake the loaves for 25 minutes, or until slightly golden. You don't want to bake them too dark. It's important to maintain a thin, crisp crust on these loaves.

MASA PIZZA CRUJIENTE (CRISPY PIZZA DOUGH)

LEVAIN BUILD

- 60 g mature sourdough starter
- 120 g bread flour
- 120 g warm water

FINAL DOUGH MIX

- 500 g bread flour
- 500 g all-purpose flour
- 670 g water
- 100 g levain
- 20 g salt
- Olive oil, for coating
- Toppings, as desired

Making pizza is one of the most forgiving processes in this book. You see, with so many styles of pizza out there, you can shape, proof, and cook the dough in a variety of successful ways. Pizza dough is one of those things you can mix and forget about for days, only to return to it and still get a delicious pizza. In this recipe, I go for a thin and crispy pan pizza that is best topped with fresh veggies, cheeses, and meats. When it comes to making pizza in a home oven, I find it best to use a sheet pan as opposed to trying to go for the Neapolitan style. The reason is, you won't be able to get the oven hot enough to achieve Neapolitan-style results. Both styles are packed with flavor and are equally delicious to me. You just can't go wrong with pizza.

———

To build the levain: In a tall jar or medium bowl, mix the mature starter, flour, and warm water until incorporated. Cover with a lid or clean kitchen towel and leave in a warm place for 3 to 4 hours, or until doubled in size. You can use your levain immediately, or refrigerate it for 12 hours to use later or the next day.

See Building and Maintaining a Levain (page 24) for more tips on how to tell if your levain is ready.

To make the final dough mix:

STEP 1: In a large bowl, mix all the final dough mix ingredients as instructed using Mixing Dough: Method 2 (page 27) until no dry flour remains.

STEP 2: Cover the dough and let rest at room temperature for 15 hours.

To shape and proof the dough:

STEP 1: Place the dough on a floured work surface, divide it in half (the dough may feel a little deflated and sticky, but this is okay), and shape each piece using a tension roll (see Shaping Dough: Method 1—Tension Roll, page 28), but don't shape them too tightly.

STEP 2: Coat 2 sheet pans with olive oil. Put each rolled dough piece onto a prepared pan.

STEP 3: Rub oil over the dough, cover it with plastic wrap, and let proof for 5 hours more.

To bake the pizza dough:

STEP 1: Preheat the oven to 500°F (250°C).

STEP 2: Rub more oil over the dough and use your hands to flatten it out, trying to cover the whole sheet pan.

STEP 3: Put your desired toppings on the pizza and bake for 25 minutes, or until you achieve a golden brown crust.

MASA PIZZA INTEGRAL (WHOLE-GRAIN PIZZA DOUGH)

YIELD: 7 PIZZAS
(250 G RAW DOUGH EACH)

LEVAIN BUILD

- 60 g mature sourdough starter
- 60 g bread flour
- 60 g whole-wheat flour
- 120 g warm water

FINAL DOUGH MIX

- 525 g whole-wheat flour
- 400 g bread flour
- 50 g spelt flour
- 25 g rye flour
- 700 g water
- 200 g levain
- 20 g salt
- Olive oil, for rubbing
- Toppings, as desired

The alternative to having a crisp, light pizza made primarily with white flour (see Masa Pizza Crujiente [Crispy Pizza Dough], page 83), is to make something more hearty and flavorful. Thus, I want to share with you my recipe for whole-grain pizza dough. I like to get creative and use as many flour types as possible to achieve a tender dough with a complex flavor. This dough works great for pizza made on a pizza stone in your home oven or outside in a wood-fired oven. If you don't have either, don't worry; you can bake them on your sheet pan or nonstick pizza pan instead. My favorite toppings to put on this dough are vegetables, such as Brussels sprouts, onions, and cherry tomatoes. For something sweeter, I opt for a fig and goat cheese combination. In any case, whatever you use will turn out to be a delicious, naturally leavened pie.

———

To build the levain: In a tall jar or medium bowl, mix the mature starter, flours, and warm water until incorporated. Cover with a lid or clean kitchen towel and leave in a warm place for 3 to 4 hours, or until doubled in size. You can use your levain immediately, or refrigerate it for 12 hours to use later or the next day.

See Building and Maintaining a Levain (page 24) for more tips on how to tell if your levain is ready.

To make the final dough mix:

STEP 1: In a large bowl, mix the flours, water, levain, and salt as instructed using Mixing Dough: Method 1 (page 26) until incorporated.

STEP 2: Cover the dough and let rest at room temperature for 4 hours.

To shape and proof the dough:

STEP 1: Line a sheet pan with parchment paper and set aside.

STEP 2: Turn the dough out on to a work surface. Divide the dough into 250-g balls (about 7) and shape each using the balling up technique (see Shaping Dough: Method 3—Balling Up, page 31). Place the dough balls on the prepared sheet pan.

STEP 3: Brush a light amount of olive oil on each dough ball and cover them with plastic wrap.

STEP 4: Refrigerate the dough for 18 hours.

To bake the pizza dough:

STEP 1: Let the dough sit on the counter for 1 to 2 hours to come to room temperature before stretching out the crusts.

STEP 2: Place a pizza stone in the oven and preheat to 500°F (250°C). If using a sheet pan or nonstick pizza pan, there is no need to preheat it inside the oven.

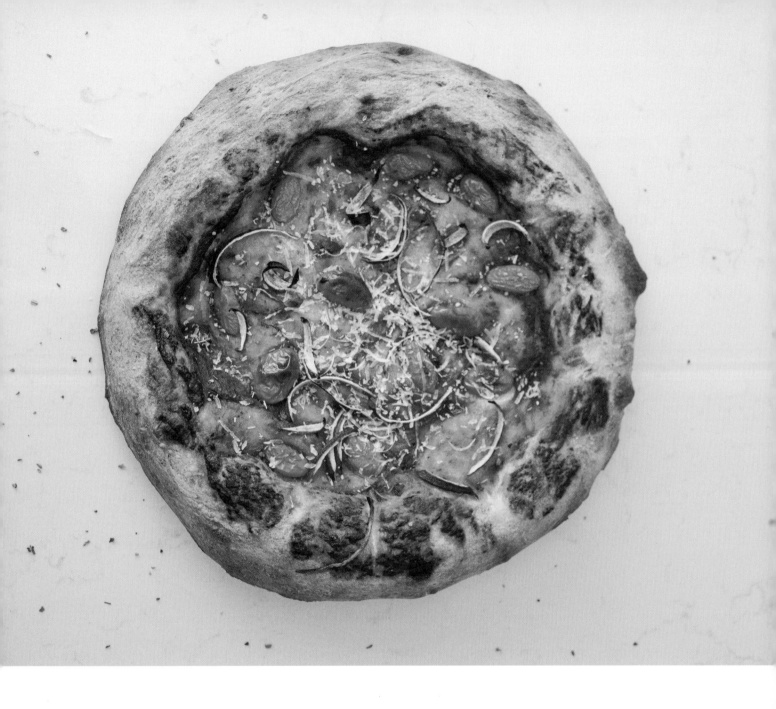

STEP 3: Place the dough on a floured work surface and stretch out your pizza dough.

STEP 4: Put your desired toppings on the pizza and bake for 15 to 20 minutes, or until you achieve your desired crust color.

⊱ **TIP**: To store extra pizza dough, wrap it in plastic wrap right from the refrigerator and put it into the freezer. Thaw in the refrigerator overnight before shaping.

MASA FOCACCIA

YIELD: 1 FOCACCIA

One of the best things about working in Italian restaurants is the abundance of bread, such as fresh focaccia. I fell in love with focaccia the very first time I tasted its salty goodness. If you're a lover of olive oil and herbs, this recipe is going to be your best friend. It's also quite different from most doughs in this book because I want to overproof this dough so it is easy to create nice peaks and valleys without too much resistance. When I'm craving a salty bread for a sandwich with crunchy textures and a moist interior, I always reach for a slice of naturally leavened focaccia.

LEVAIN BUILD

- 50 g mature sourdough starter
- 50 g bread flour
- 50 g whole-wheat flour
- 65 g warm water

FINAL DOUGH MIX

- 800 g bread flour
- 200 g whole-wheat flour
- 700 g water
- 100 g olive oil
- 100 g levain
- 84 g light brown sugar
- 20 g salt
- Olive oil, for preparing the pan and dough
- Sea salt, for sprinkling
- Toppings, as desired

To build the levain: In a tall jar or medium bowl, mix the mature starter, flours, and warm water until incorporated. Cover with a lid or clean kitchen towel and leave in a warm place for 3 to 4 hours, or until doubled in size. You can use your levain immediately, or refrigerate it for 12 hours to use later or the next day.

See Building and Maintaining a Levain (page 24) for more tips on how to tell if your levain is ready.

To make the final dough mix:

STEP 1: In a large bowl, mix all the final dough mix ingredients as instructed using Mixing Dough: Method 1 (page 26) until incorporated.

STEP 2: Cover the dough and let sit at room temperature overnight, or up to 12 hours.

To shape and proof the dough:

STEP 1: Coat a sheet pan with olive oil and set aside.

STEP 2: Put the dough on a floured work surface and shape the whole amount of dough using a tension roll (see Shaping Dough: Method 1—Tension Roll, page 28). Don't roll it too tightly—a nice loose cylinder works great here. Place the dough on the prepared sheet pan.

STEP 3: Cover the dough generously with olive oil and a sprinkle of sea salt.

STEP 4: Cover the dough with plastic wrap and let proof for 3 hours, or until it is spongy and jiggly when you shake the tray.

To poach and bake the focaccia:

STEP 1: Preheat the oven to 420°F (215.5°C).

STEP 2: Drizzle more olive oil over the dough. Using your fingers on both hands (Don't use the very tips of your fingers; use the finger print area. Pretend you are playing the piano!), poke rows of craters into the dough.

STEP 3: Add your toppings! My favorite combination is a sprinkle of oregano and rosemary, cherry tomatoes, and sea salt.

STEP 4: Bake the focaccia for 15 to 20 minutes, or until you achieve your desired crust color.

WHOLE-GRAIN
PITA BREAD

LEVAIN BUILD

- 50 g mature sourdough starter
- 100 g bread flour
- 100 g warm water

FINAL DOUGH MIX

- 250 g bread flour
- 50 g spelt flour
- 200 g whole-wheat flour
- 315 g water
- 100 g levain
- 10 g salt
- Oils, for rubbing

My first experience with pita bread was that of confusion, as I was under the impression I was about to eat a tortilla. Then, my friend took a knife and sliced through the bread to expose a perfectly hollow interior. Soon, mixed greens, meats, and veggies were stuffed into it and a little bit of oil and vinegar was drizzled on top. As I got older, however, I realized how normal and abundant pita bread is. You can find it everywhere, and for good reason. It is a light bread that is designed specifically to hold various fillings. At the same time, you can also rip warm pita to bits and dip it into delicious spreads such as hummus. Adding whole grains and sourdough starter was an obvious choice to add to my repertoire and I can't wait for you to try this version.

———

To build the levain: In a tall jar or medium bowl, mix the mature starter, flour, and warm water until incorporated. Cover with a lid or clean kitchen towel and leave in a warm place for 3 to 4 hours, or until doubled in size. You can use your levain immediately, or refrigerate it for 12 hours to use later or the next day.

See Building and Maintaining a Levain (page 24) for more tips on how to tell if your levain is ready.

To make the final dough mix:

STEP 1: In a large bowl, mix the flours, water, levain, and salt as instructed using Mixing Dough: Method 2 (page 27) until incorporated and no dry flour remains.

STEP 2: Cover the dough and let ferment at room temperature for 6 hours.

To shape and proof the dough:

STEP 1: Line a sheet pan with parchment paper and set aside.

STEP 2: Divide the dough into 4 pieces and shape each piece using the rounding technique (see Shaping Dough: Method 2—Rounding, page 30). Place the dough on the prepared sheet pan.

STEP 3: Apply some oil to the dough. Cover the dough with plastic wrap and refrigerate overnight, or up to 12 hours.

To bake the pizza dough:

You'll need a very hot cast iron skillet, pizza stone, or sheet pan to bake these guys so they puff up nicely. If using cast iron, there is no need to apply the lid.

STEP 1: Place your baking vessel into the oven and preheat the oven to 500°F (250°C).

STEP 2: Flour a work surface. Place the dough on it and, using a rolling pin, roll each dough ball into a very thin circle.

STEP 3: Place your pitas onto the baking vessel and bake for 10 to 15 minutes, or until nice even brown spots appear, flipping them halfway through the baking time. After a minute or so, your pita bread should puff up.

TORTILLAS DE HARINA (FLOUR TORTILLAS)

LEVAIN BUILD

- 15 g mature sourdough starter
- 50 g bread flour
- 50 g whole-wheat flour
- 100 g warm water

FINAL DOUGH MIX

- 125 g warm coconut milk
- 100 g levain
- 400 g all-purpose flour
- 100 g warm water
- 25 g coconut oil
- 25 g vegetable oil, plus more for kneading and oiling
- 5 g kosher salt
- 1 egg

My mother's recipe yields the absolute best tortilla I have ever eaten. She uses baking soda and eggs, which are very traditional in tortillas to help them *inflar*, or puff up, while cooking. If your tortillas are not puffing up a bit while they cook, you will get that look of disapproval from a Honduran mother! I have opted to use my sourdough starter in place of those two items to achieve the same consistency and make a more easily digestible, flavorful, and healthier tortilla. In addition, the Honduran secret weapon to a good tortilla is coconut milk. (If you have this book, I suspect your pantry is stocked with coconut milk anyway.) I learned how to make tortillas from watching my mom over and over again, but I'm still searching for perfection in my own recipe.

———

To build the levain: In a tall jar or medium bowl, mix the mature starter, flours, and warm water until incorporated. Cover with a lid or clean kitchen towel and leave in a warm place for 12 to 14 hours. You want to catch the levain right as it begins to fall and lose potency.

See Building and Maintaining a Levain (page 24) for more tips on how to tell if your levain is ready.

To make the final dough mix:

STEP 1: In a large bowl, combine the warm coconut milk and levain to dissolve.

STEP 2: Add the flour, warm water, coconut oil, vegetable oil, and salt and, using your hands, mix everything as instructed using Mixing Dough: Method 2 (page 27) until incorporated.

STEP 3: Turn the dough out on to a work surface and knead it with the palm of your hand. If the dough is a bit sticky, don't worry; it will come together through the kneading process. Don't add more flour as this will make the tortillas too dry. Add small amounts of vegetable oil while kneading to help smooth out the dough and create a nice elastic surface.

STEP 4: Let the dough rest for 30 minutes after kneading.

(continued)

To shape and proof the dough:

Because tortillas are not exactly leavened, they don't require much in terms of fermentation or proofing.

STEP 1: Shape the dough into a log and cut it into 6 even sections.

STEP 2: Using the palm of your hand, but with your fingers around the edges of each piece, shape the dough into round balls using the balling up technique (see Shaping Dough: Method 3—Balling Up, page 31).

STEP 3: Oil a cutting board and place the dough balls on it. Cover the dough and let proof for 10 minutes.

STEP 4: Once you are ready to shape your tortillas, heat a large skillet over medium heat.

STEP 5: Oil a large plate and use the plate to flatten the tortillas. All you have to do is put a bit of oil on the plate and press with the tips of your fingers to push the edge of the dough to the edge of the plate.

To cook the tortillas:

STEP 1: When your skillet is hot and you see a bit of smoke rising, lower the temperature a bit, to about medium-low. Cook each tortilla for 4 minutes per side. Make sure your pan is up to temperature so when the tortilla hits the pan you begin to see small bubbles within the first 45 seconds.

STEP 2: Transfer the cooked tortillas to a paper towel to rest. Fill them with anything and enjoy!

To store:

Let the tortillas cool completely before putting them into a zip-top or paper bag, and refrigerate. When ready to eat, warm them up on the stove in a skillet.

❧ **TIP**: If you want to use these right way, fill them with creamy red beans and crumbly, salty cheese. This is what is called a *baleada sencilla* in Honduras. The best!

"IF YOUR TORTILLAS
ARE NOT PUFFING
UP A BIT WHILE
THEY COOK,
YOU WILL GET
THAT LOOK OF
DISAPPROVAL
FROM A HONDURAN
MOTHER!"

ENRICHED BREADS

Ah, the good stuff. I know, rustic breads have a certain appeal and nutritional value, but, hey, we need to indulge a little, don't we? Enter enriched breads. The way I define an enriched bread is based not just on the ingredients, but also the overall look and characteristics of the bread. I believe that if a mix has a few of the following ingredients, then it is enriched: milk, eggs, fat or oil (butter, olive oil, etc.), and some type of sugar (honey or brown sugar). However, I also believe that the appearance, texture, and smell of the bread play a part as well. When I smell the beautiful aroma of Choco Pan de Coco (page 99) and taste the soft, smooth, delicate interior, I know that recipe belongs in this section. Not only are these breads extremely fun to make, but they are even more fun to share with others. Most people don't equate the word *sourdough* with soft, sweet loaves such as brioche and monkey bread. But as many of you who follow my blog have discovered, you can, indeed, leaven your delicious enriched loaves with your sourdough starter!

CHOCO PAN DE COCO

LEVAIN BUILD

- 60 g mature sourdough starter
- 120 g bread flour
- 110 g warm water

FINAL DOUGH MIX

- 200 g coconut milk
- 100 g water
- 225 g bread flour
- 225 g all-purpose flour
- 200 g levain
- 125 g shredded coconut, plus more for topping (preferably unsweetened, but if all you have is sweetened, that will work, too)
- 50 g cocoa powder
- 50 g bittersweet chocolate chips, plus more for topping
- 30 g unsalted butter, or coconut oil, plus more for preparing the pan
- 30 g light brown sugar
- 10 g salt

I was pleasantly surprised when I saw how many readers made the pan de coco recipe on my blog. This bread truly represents what I'm all about as a baker, as its simplicity goes unnoticed due to the complexities of aroma and flavor. We crave the moment when this bread is piping hot out of the oven, with the subtle aroma of sweet coconut and a pinch of whole-grain flour permeating the air, while our eyes are hypnotized by crumbling toasted shards of coconut, we carelessly burn our hands just a bit to open up the pillowy soft, warm bread. This version brings new flavors, colors, and textures to my classic recipe. If you can't guess by the name, chocolate lovers will be pleased!

———

To build the levain: In a tall jar or medium bowl, mix the mature starter, flour, and warm water until incorporated. Cover with a lid or clean kitchen towel and leave in a warm place for 3 to 4 hours, or until doubled in size. You can use your levain immediately, or refrigerate it for 12 hours to use later or the next day.

See Building and Maintaining a Levain (page 24) for more tips on how to tell if your levain is ready.

To make the final dough mix:

STEP 1: In a large, microwave-safe bowl, combine the coconut milk and water. Microwave briefly to warm slightly.

STEP 2: Add the levain and remaining ingredients and mix as instructed using Mixing Dough: Method 2 (page 27) until incorporated.

STEP 3: Cover the dough and let ferment at room temperature for 4 hours. Refrigerate for 12 hours more.

To shape and proof the dough:

STEP 1: Coat a loaf tin with coconut oil or butter and set aside.

STEP 2: Place the dough on a floured work surface, divide it into 6 pieces, and shape each piece using the balling up technique (see Shaping Dough: Method 3—Balling Up, page 31). Place the pieces in the prepared tin in 2 rows of 3.

STEP 3: Cover the dough and let proof at room temperature for 3 to 4 hours.

To bake the bread:

STEP 1: Preheat the oven to 375°F (190°C).

STEP 2: Sprinkle the loaf with more bittersweet chocolate and shredded coconut, as desired.

STEP 3: Bake the bread for 35 minutes, or until golden brown. You may need to rotate your pan half way through the bake. Some ovens have hotspots to watch for and you will learn over time as you bake how evenly your oven bakes things. Hot spots are typically at the back corners of the oven, so if these begin to get dark before other parts of the bread, you should rotate the loaf to get an even color.

❧ **TIP**: Don't forget to open up the loaf when it is hot out of the oven. It makes for great pictures!

HONEY OAT TIN LOAF

LEVAIN BUILD

- 50 g mature sourdough starter
- 100 g whole-wheat flour
- 80 g warm water

FINAL DOUGH MIX

- 700 g whole-wheat flour
- 100 g bread flour
- 200 g all-purpose flour
- 700 g water
- 20 g salt
- 200 g levain
- 100 g raw old-fashioned rolled oats, plus more for topping
- 75 g honey, plus more for drizzling
- Olive oil, for preparing the bowl

I always craved a recipe for a tin loaf that had a deep, whole-meal flavor to it. Like most people, store-bought sliced bread was common in my home, and what I considered whole-wheat bread growing up has been completely flipped upside down since I started making my own sourdough bread. Using a good quality whole-wheat flour is the key to making a loaf that packs a punch; the addition of honey and oats gives it an extra push of flavor. I like to take this recipe a step further by lathering the dough with honey and oats before baking—enough honey so it drips down the tin to create a caramelized crust on the sides. I used to prefer different breads to whole-wheat bread growing up, yet my tastes have changed dramatically and I often reach for my whole-wheat flour first when craving a simple loaf of bread at home.

————

To build the levain: In a tall jar or medium bowl, mix the mature starter, flour, and warm water until incorporated. Cover with a lid or clean kitchen towel and leave in a warm place for 3 to 4 hours, or until doubled in size. You can use your levain immediately, or refrigerate it for 12 hours to use later or the next day.

See Building and Maintaining a Levain (page 24) for more tips on how to tell if your levain is ready.

To make the final dough mix:

STEP 1: In a large bowl, mix all the final dough mix ingredients as instructed using Mixing Dough: Method 2 (page 27) until no dry flour remains. Once the ingredients are just combined, turn the dough out on to a work surface and knead it with your palm until smooth.

STEP 2: Coat a large, clean bowl with oil and transfer the dough to it. Cover the dough and let rise at room temperature for 4 hours. You do not need to stretch or fold this dough during the initial rise. Refrigerate the bowl, covered and without shaping, for 12 hours.

To shape and proof the dough:

STEP 1: Lightly coat 2 loaf tins with oil and set aside.

STEP 2: Lightly flour a work surface. Remove the dough from the fridge, place it on the work surface, and divide it in half. Shape each piece using a tension roll (see Shaping Dough: Method 1—Tension Roll, page 28). Put each loaf into one of the prepared tins.

STEP 3: Cover the dough and let proof at room temperature for 3 to 4 hours, or until soft to the touch and jiggly when you move the pan.

To bake the bread:

STEP 1: Preheat the oven to 475°F (240°C).

STEP 2: Liberally drizzle the loaves with honey and coat each with a handful of oats. Score your loaves with a knife by making 2 separate Xs on each loaf.

STEP 3: Bake your loaves for 30 minutes, or until golden brown on top. You want to get a crisp caramelization of the honey on the top and sides of the loaves.

STEP 4: Let cool completely if you want to slice the bread for sandwich use.

BANANAS FOSTER
SOURDOUGH

LEVAIN BUILD

- 60 g mature sourdough starter
- 120 g bread flour
- 110 g warm water

FINAL DOUGH MIX

- 240 g warm whole milk
- 210 g levain
- 75 g light brown sugar
- 1 egg
- 4 g honey
- 2 g vanilla extract
- 500 g bread flour
- 100 g unsalted butter, at room temperature, plus more for preparing the loaf tin
- 25 g ground cinnamon
- 4 g salt

BANANAS FOSTER FILLING AND TOPPING

- 40 g unsalted butter, divided
- 40 g light brown sugar, divided
- 5 g ground cinnamon, divided
- 4 g vanilla extract, divided
- 2 ripe bananas
- 4 g dark rum, divided

It's no surprise New Orleans has a classic dessert made with bananas, given the history of the banana trade in the city. However, not everyone has had the pleasure of eating bananas Foster prepared tableside. The smell of bananas caramelized in brown sugar, butter, and rum? Pure heaven. How about we just put this filling inside and on top of a pillow-y soft, naturally leavened dough? Even more heavenly. I couldn't resist jazzing up some dough with this golden brown goodness.

To build the levain: In a tall jar or medium bowl, mix the mature starter, flour, and warm water until incorporated. Cover with a lid or clean kitchen towel and leave in a warm place for 3 to 4 hours, or until doubled in size. You can use your levain immediately, or refrigerate it for 12 hours to use later or the next day.

See Building and Maintaining a Levain (page 24) for more tips on how to tell if your levain is ready.

To make the final dough mix:

STEP 1: In a large bowl, whisk the warm milk, levain, brown sugar, egg, honey, and vanilla until incorporated, but still kind of lumpy.

STEP 2: Add the flour, butter, cinnamon, and salt. Using your hands, mix the ingredients until the dough starts to come together. Once it does not feel too wet, turn it out on to a work surface and knead the dough (see Mixing Dough: Method 2, page 27). Transfer the dough to a clean bowl.

STEP 3: Cover the dough and let rest at room temperature for 4 hours. The dough may not fully double in size; that's okay. What you're looking for is a smooth surface, some bubbles, and a subtly sweet smell. Refrigerate the dough, still covered, for 8 to 10 hours, ideally overnight.

To make the bananas Foster filling and topping:

You will make two separate items: the filling that will go inside the dough before proofing and the topping that will be drizzled over the bread. One hour before the cold fermentation is up, make the filling using half the filling and topping ingredients.

STEP 1: In a saucepan over medium heat, combine half each of the butter, brown sugar, cinnamon, and vanilla. Cook for 2 to 3 minutes until it starts to thicken.

STEP 2: Mash one of the bananas and stir it into the butter-sugar mixture.

STEP 3: Stir in half the rum. Let the filling simmer on low heat for 5 minutes. Turn off the heat, transfer the mixture to an aluminum bowl, and place it in the freezer for 5 minutes before transferring to the fridge.

(continued)

STEP 4: Repeat this process with the remaining ingredients, but instead of mashing the remaining banana, cut it lengthwise into long slices.

To shape and proof the dough:

STEP 1: Coat a loaf tin with butter and set aside.

STEP 2: Turn the dough out on to a floured work surface and pat it down. Using a rolling pin, roll out a rectangle about ½ inch (1 cm) thick.

STEP 3: Use a knife to trim the rounded edges. Remove the filling (with the mashed banana) from the fridge and use a spatula to spread it evenly over the dough. Starting at the longer end of the rectangle, roll the dough into a cylinder and put it into the prepared loaf tin.

STEP 4: Place the banana slices on top of the dough and drizzle it with the remaining sauce.

STEP 5: Cover the dough with a plastic bag and let proof in a warm area for 4 to 6 hours.

To bake the bread:

STEP 1: About 30 minutes before the end of your proof, preheat the oven to 375°F (190°C). You'll know the dough is almost ready when it's popping out of the tin and springy to the touch. If it's ready and you haven't preheated the oven, don't worry! The extra proof is always welcome with enriched sourdough loaves.

STEP 2: Bake the bread for 35 to 40 minutes, or until golden brown and firm in the center. You'll want to make sure this bakes all the way through, and my sure sign of this loaf being completely done is a nice, dark color on top. I actually sometimes like to burn the loaf just a bit for some extra flavor—but not everyone is into that.

STEP 3: Remove the loaf from the oven and turn it out of the pan and onto a cutting board or wire cooling rack. It's super important that this one cools before you cut it so it can finish cooking around the filling areas. Enjoy!

❧ **TIP**: To make a non-alcoholic version of this bread, you can exclude the rum or cook it longer to make sure the alcohol is cooked off. You could also use apple or pineapple juice instead of rum.

CINNY RAISIN BAGELS

LEVAIN BUILD

- 100 g mature sourdough starter
- 200 g bread flour
- 200 g warm water

FINAL DOUGH MIX

- 500 g warm water
- 400 g levain
- 35 g honey
- 1 kg bread flour
- 200 g raisins (golden, mixed, or regular)
- 40 g ground cinnamon
- 20 g salt

FOR BOILING

- 100 g honey
- 14 g baking soda

My dad would often bring home cinnamon-raisin bagels from the store, usually when the bodega was closed and we couldn't get *semitas* (see page 117). It was his favorite flavor and, oddly enough, he did not warm or toast them. He did not eat them with anything, and he did not even slice the bagel in half. He would simply grab one and bite into it. I was never a fan of the store-bought ones, so I decided to make a high quality cinnamon-raisin bagel that both my dad and I would love. Perhaps you'll be tempted to taking a huge bite out of one of these when you're done.

To build the levain: In a tall jar or medium bowl, mix the mature starter, flour, and warm water until incorporated. Cover with a lid or clean kitchen towel and leave in a warm place for 3 to 4 hours, or until doubled in size. You can use your levain immediately, or refrigerate it for 12 hours to use later or the next day.

See Building and Maintaining a Levain (page 24) for more tips on how to tell if your levain is ready.

To make the final dough mix:

STEP 1: In a large bowl, using a fork or your clean hands, mix the warm water, levain, and honey.

STEP 2: Add the flour, raisins, cinnamon, and salt and mix with your hands to combine. The mixture will feel a bit dry, but continue to mix and squeeze (see Mixing Dough: Method 2, page 27) to finish working the dough until you have a smooth surface.

STEP 3: Cover the dough and let rest at room temperature for 4 hours.

To shape and proof the dough:

STEP 1: Line a sheet pan with parchment paper and set aside.

STEP 2: Divide the dough into 140-g pieces (about 14) and lightly shape each piece into a small, tight cylinder about 3 inches (7.5 cm) long. Place the dough pieces on the prepared sheet pan and let rest for 30 minutes. Don't worry about spacing, or whether the dough touches while resting.

(continued)

STEP 3: It's time to roll your bagels! Take one dough piece and place it in front on your work surface horizontally, so the top and bottom of the cylinder are facing to the sides. Starting with your palm in the middle of the cylinder, roll it up and down to elongate the piece. As it gets longer, use both hands. Place each hand on one of the edges, as the center is already smaller. Roll the edges back and forth, with your thumbs touching and your other fingers extending in the opposite direction of your thumbs. Once you have a long cylinder that extends from the tip of your pinky on one hand to the tip of the other pinky while your thumbs are touching (about 8 inches, or 20 cm, long), you can stop rolling.

STEP 4: Place the palm of your hand on one side, with the edge of your hand meeting the edge of the cylinder. Pick up the dough, with your fingers wrapping around it. Use your other hand to flip the other side of the dough around the top of your hand so that it connects into your palm.

STEP 5: Once the two edges connect and you have the bagel shaped around your hand, press the connected edges down onto the work surface and give it a few rolls back and forth to seal the circular bagel shape. Place the shaped bagel on the prepared sheet pan. Repeat, shaping the remaining bagels. Space your bagels out well so they can proof without touching. I usually do 3 by 4 on a half sheet pan.

STEP 6: Let the bagels proof at room temperature for 30 minutes. Cover with plastic wrap and refrigerate for at least 15 hours.

To boil and bake the bagels:

STEP 1: Preheat the oven to 450°F (230°C).

STEP 2: Bring a large pot three-fourths full of water to a boil over high heat. Add the honey and baking soda. Once you get a rolling boil, lower the heat so you have a gentler boil.

STEP 3: A few at a time, boil the bagels straight from the fridge, for 45 seconds per side. (If your bagels don't float after the first minute, they need to proof longer. Leave them at room temperature for an hour or so.) Use a wooden spoon to flip the bagels and transfer them back to the sheet pan, spaced 3 by 4.

STEP 4: Put the boiled bagels into the oven and bake for 12 to 15 minutes. You're looking for a dark color and caramelized raisins! You don't want to let them sit out too long or they will collapse. While the bagels bake, continue to boil the remaining bagels for baking.

STEP 5: Let your bagels cool, if you want, and cut them in half and enjoy! Although, I suggest eating these just like my dad did.

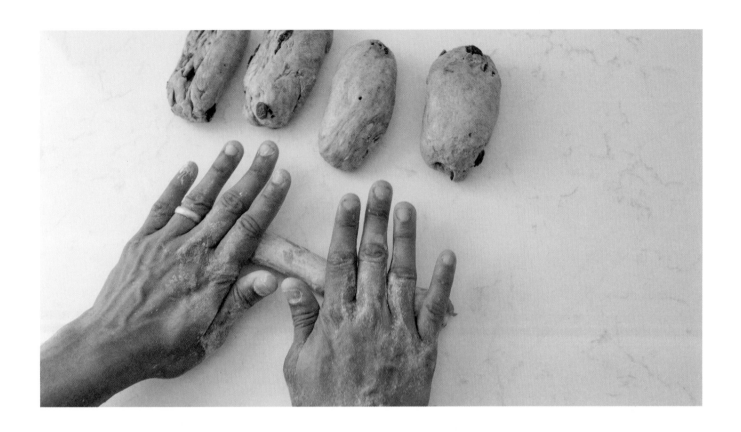

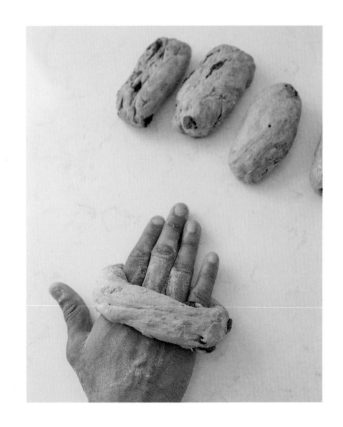

PECAN PRALINE MONKEY BREAD

YIELD: 1 LOAF

LEVAIN BUILD

- 60 g mature sourdough starter
- 120 g bread flour
- 110 g warm water

FINAL DOUGH MIX

- 210 g levain
- 200 g whole milk
- 100 g water
- 2 eggs
- 80 g light brown sugar
- 50 g melted unsalted butter
- 2 g vanilla extract
- 300 g all-purpose flour
- 200 g bread flour
- 5 g salt

PECAN PRALINES

- 200 g evaporated milk
- 200 g granulated sugar
- 200 g light brown sugar
- 80 g unsalted butter
- 3 g salt
- 2 g vanilla extract
- 300 g pecan halves

BUTTERY GLAZE

- 150 g granulated sugar
- 10 g ground cinnamon
- 3 g ground nutmeg
- 100 g melted unsalted butter, cooled, divided, plus more for coating the pan
- 100 g light brown sugar
- 5 g vanilla extract

Who can complain when there is a pile of sweet, sticky bread on the table that is literally meant to be ripped apart and eaten with your hands? This, to me, sounds like the ideal way to eat bread. To sweeten the deal, this monkey bread is coated with crushed fresh pecan pralines you can make in minutes. I'm a fan of the classic New Orleans pecan praline because of the history behind it. It is said that African American women used ever-abundant Louisiana pecans instead of the traditional almonds, creating something so delicious that pecan pralines became the New Orleans standard. As a baker, remember how important it is to use what you have and appreciate it!

———

To build the levain: In a tall jar or medium bowl, mix the mature starter, flour, and warm water until incorporated. Cover with a lid or clean kitchen towel and leave in a warm place for 3 to 4 hours, or until doubled in size. You can use your levain immediately, or refrigerate it for 12 hours to use later or the next day.

See Building and Maintaining a Levain (page 24) for more tips on how to tell if your levain is ready.

To make the final dough mix:

STEP 1: In a large bowl, whisk the levain, milk, water, eggs, melted butter, brown sugar, and vanilla until combined.

STEP 2: Add the flours and salt. Using your hands, mix the ingredients as instructed using Mixing Dough: Method 2 (page 27) to finish developing this dough.

STEP 3: Cover the dough and let rise at room temperature for 4 hours. Refrigerate the dough overnight, or for 10 hours.

To make the pecan pralines:

STEP 1: Line a sheet pan with parchment paper and set aside.

STEP 2: In a saucepan over medium heat, combine the evaporated milk, sugars, butter, salt, and vanilla and bring to a boil while stirring constantly. Once you see the mixture boiling and bubbling, remove it from the heat and add the pecans. Stir vigorously for a couple of minutes.

STEP 3: Drop tablespoon-size portions of the mixture onto the prepared sheet pan. Let cool completely before crumbling the pralines.

To make the buttery glaze:

STEP 1: In a small bowl, stir together the granulated sugar, cinnamon, and nutmeg.

STEP 2: Place 50 g of melted butter in a small bowl and set aside.

(continued)

To shape and proof the dough:

STEP 1: Turn the dough out on to a floured work surface, divide it into 25-g balls (about 50), and shape each piece using the balling up technique (see Shaping Dough: Method 3—Balling Up, page 31).

STEP 2: Coat a 9½-inch (23 cm) Bundt pan with butter and crumbled pralines. Save a little crumbled praline for sprinkling the finished dough.

STEP 3: Dip each dough ball into the melted butter and then into the spiced sugar mixture. Place the coated dough balls into the prepared cake pan.

To finish the buttery glaze:

STEP 1: In a medium bowl, whisk the remaining 50 g of melted butter, the brown sugar, and the vanilla until smooth. Pour the glaze over the dough balls.

STEP 2: Sprinkle the bread with the reserved crumbled praline.

STEP 3: Cover the bread and let proof at room temperature for 4 hours.

To bake the monkey bread:

STEP 1: Preheat the oven to 375°F (190°C).

STEP 2: Bake the monkey bread for 35 minutes, or until golden brown.

STEP 3: Let cool for a few minutes and then flip the Bundt pan over on a cutting board. This bread is best served warm out of the oven!

"AS A BAKER,
REMEMBER HOW
IMPORTANT IT
IS TO USE WHAT
YOU HAVE AND
APPRECIATE IT."

SEMITAS DE YEMA

LEVAIN BUILD

- 100 g mature sourdough starter
- 150 g bread flour
- 50 g whole-wheat flour
- 200 g warm water

FINAL DOUGH MIX

- 500 g bread flour
- 500 g all-purpose flour
- 200 g egg yolks
- 250 g granulated sugar
- 250 g unsalted butter, at room temperature
- 100 g water
- 350 g levain
- 5 g salt

LA CUBIERTA

- 200 g all-purpose flour, plus more as needed
- 150 g coconut oil
- 100 g granulated sugar

Almost every day after school, I would wait for my dad to bring home a bag of *semitas* from the local Honduran bodega. My parents enjoyed afternoon coffee more often than not, and as these are best dipped in hot coffee, it was a ritual of sorts for us to enjoy *semitas* with warm beverages on the porch. I didn't drink coffee when I was young, so warm milk or hot chocolate was my go-to. Even when we moved to a New Orleans suburb, there were pockets of Central American people and markets, so finding these classic treats was easy.

This bread is a semisweet, dense brioche-style bread capped with a crisp mixture of oil and sugar and is best served with a warm cup of coffee. Having proper *semitas* is akin to having a proper croissant—the moment you know you are going to eat one is filled with a happiness that can only be satisfied by eating as many as possible.

———

To build the levain: In a tall jar or medium bowl, mix the mature starter, flours, and warm water until incorporated. Cover with a lid or clean kitchen towel and leave in a warm place for 3 to 4 hours until doubled. You can use your levain immediately, or refrigerate it for 12 hours to use later or the next day.

See Building and Maintaining a Levain (page 24) for more tips on how to tell if your levain is ready.

To make the final dough mix:

STEP 1: In a large bowl, mix all the final dough mix ingredients, squeezing them with both hands until a dough starts to come together (see Mixing Dough: Method 2, page 27 for more instruction).

STEP 2: Cover the dough with a clean kitchen cloth or plastic bag and let ferment at room temperature for 6 hours. Refrigerate the dough for 12 hours.

To make la cubierta:

STEP 1: Remove the dough from the fridge and let it sit on the counter while you make la cubierta.

STEP 2: In a medium bowl, combine the flour, coconut oil, and granulated sugar. Whisk rapidly until you have a soft, crumbly mixture. You want it to be more dry than wet, so, if needed, add a bit more flour. Turn the mixture out on to a work surface and gently knead it into a ball. Set aside.

(continued)

To shape and proof the dough:

STEP 1: Line a sheet pan with parchment paper and set aside.

STEP 2: Divide the dough into 120-g pieces (about 16) and shape each one using the balling up technique (see Shaping Dough: Method 3—Balling Up, page 31).

STEP 3: Take a small handful of the cubierta mixture (around 20 g, but you don't need to measure); make a flat disk with the mixture and place it on top of each rounded dough ball. Place the dough rounds on the prepared sheet pan.

STEP 4: Proof the dough at room temperature for 4 hours following Proofing Dough: Method 3—Loaf Tin/Sheet Pan (page 33) until you see some cracking in the cubierta and growth in size.

STEP 5: You'll know the dough is ready to bake when the cubierta is cracking; however, it may not always crack. Use a razor blade or knife to cut some designs into the cubierta before baking, as desired.

To bake the bread:

STEP 1: Preheat the oven to 375°F (190°C).

STEP 2: Bake the semitas on the sheet pan for 30 minutes, or until golden brown.

STEP 3: Let cool for 15 or 20 minutes to ensure they are cooked all the way through before eating. Remember, these are best enjoyed with your favorite cup of coffee. Dip it in and enjoy.

CHALLAH

LEVAIN BUILD

- 100 g mature sourdough starter
- 200 g bread flour
- 150 g warm water

FINAL DOUGH MIX

- 400 g water
- 350 g levain
- 2 eggs
- 1 egg yolk
- 25 g olive oil, plus more for brushing
- 700 g bread flour
- 200 g all-purpose flour
- 100 g spelt flour
- 100 g light brown sugar
- 15 g salt

EGG WASH

- 1 egg
- Splash water
- Pinch salt

I didn't really know what Shabbat was until I moved to Miami, and to take that one step further, I didn't know what it meant to have challah. I mean, I knew what challah was. But I never understood what it *meant*. Now, I have a great appreciation for challah as I have lived in a city where it is a treasure, and it's a treasure for a good reason. In my many challah tests, I found that adding a pinch of spelt flour was the key to a well-balanced and delicious loaf. Challah is a dense, but fluffy, bread that is enjoyable to eat on its own. I hope you make and enjoy this recipe for your holiday, or any occasion!

―――――

To build the levain: In a tall jar or medium bowl, mix the mature starter, flour, and warm water until incorporated. Cover with a lid or clean kitchen towel and leave in a warm place for 3 to 4 hours, or until doubled in size. You can use your levain immediately, or refrigerate it for 12 hours to use later or the next day.

See Building and Maintaining a Levain (page 24) for more tips on how to tell if your levain is ready.

To make the final dough mix:

STEP 1: In a large bowl, combine the water and levain to dissolve the levain.

STEP 2: Add the eggs, egg yolk, and oil. Whisk to combine.

STEP 3: In a medium bowl, whisk the flours, brown sugar, and salt until evenly blended. Add these dry ingredients to the egg mixture and mix as instructed using Mixing Dough: Method 2 (page 27) until incorporated. Knead this dough for a good 10 to 15 minutes.

STEP 4: Cover the dough and let ferment at room temperature for 4 hours. Refrigerate the dough for 15 hours more.

To shape and proof the dough:

STEP 1: Line a sheet pan with parchment paper and set aside.

STEP 2: Remove the dough from the fridge and let rest at room temperature for 30 minutes.

STEP 3: Turn the dough out on to a floured work surface, divide it into 5 pieces, and shape each piece use the balling up technique (see Shaping Dough: Method 3—Balling Up, page 31). Let the dough balls rest for 10 minutes.

STEP 4: Elongate each dough ball into a long, skinny tube using the palm of your hand to rock the dough back and forth, applying a little pressure. When it gets long enough, use two hands. The final pieces should be about 15 inches (38 cm) long, but don't worry if they are shorter if your dough is not as strong.

(continued on page 124)

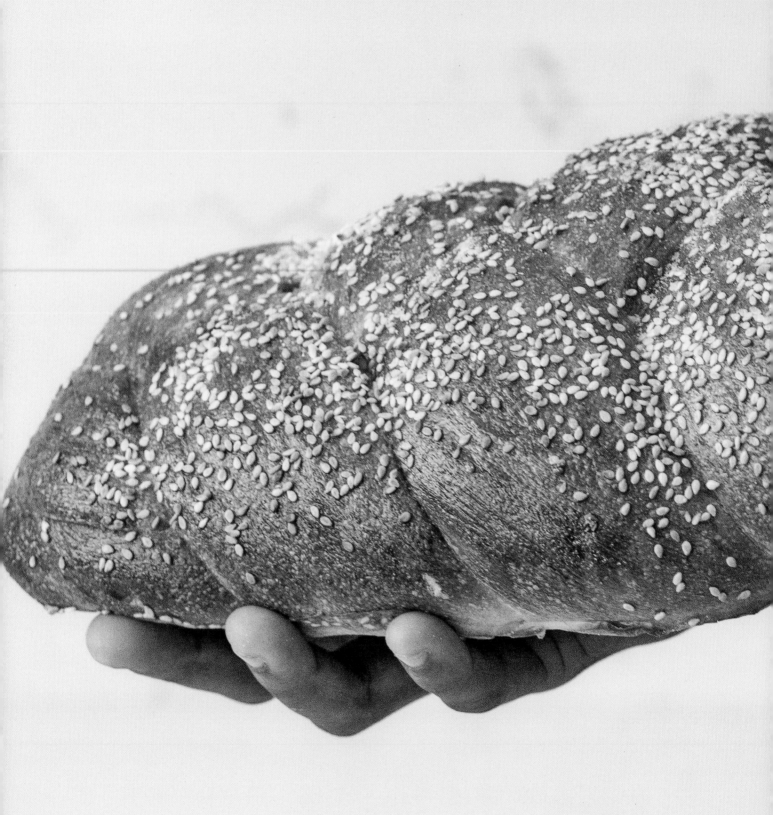

STEP 5: Braid your challah: Pinch all the strands together at one end. Move the strands from the right into the center. Repeat with the left side. Get creative here and don't worry if it doesn't look perfect. Place your braided challah on the prepared sheet pan. Using a pastry brush, coat the challah with a little bit of oil.

STEP 6: Cover the challah with plastic wrap and let proof at room temperature for 3 hours.

To make the egg wash:

In a small bowl, whisk the egg, water, and salt until blended. Set aside.

To bake the bread:

STEP 1: Preheat the oven to 375°F (190°C).

STEP 2: Using a pastry brush, coat the challah loaf with the egg wash.

STEP 3: Bake for 30 to 35 minutes until golden brown on top.

TIP: You can coat your challah with sesame or poppy seeds. Simply sprinkle these onto your loaf after egg washing and put into the oven.

WHOLE-GRAIN BRIOCHE BUNS

LEVAIN BUILD

- 75 g mature sourdough starter
- 100 g bread flour
- 50 g whole-wheat flour
- 150 g warm water

FINAL DOUGH MIX

- 175 g eggs
- 90 g cold water
- 250 g levain
- 100 g light brown sugar
- 6 g honey
- 6 g grated lemon zest
- 6 g grated orange zest
- 1 g vanilla extract
- 175 g unsalted butter, at room temperature, cubed
- 350 g bread flour
- 100 g whole-wheat flour
- 50 g spelt flour
- 6 g salt
- Sesame seeds or poppy seeds, for topping (optional)
- Boiling water, for steaming

The multi-purpose nature of brioche is a phenomenon worth exploring. Soft, flaky, and buttery bread is something every household should always have on hand to enjoy. Although I love a classic brioche made with all white flour and pumped full of sweet cream or fillings, I also love incorporating whole grains into my brioche mix. I prefer shaping this brioche into buns and using them for more savory purposes, such as sandwiches and burgers. Without a doubt, you can also eat these plain as a snack. You loved the sweet brioche recipe on my blog, and I am certain this one will give you great pleasure as well.

———

To build the levain: In a tall or medium bowl, mix the mature starter, flours, and warm water until incorporated. Cover with a lid or clean kitchen towel and leave in a warm place for 3 to 4 hours until doubled. You can use your levain immediately, or refrigerate it for 12 hours to use at a later time or the next day.

See Building and Maintaining a Levain (page 24) for more tips on how to tell if your levain is ready.

To make the final dough mix:

STEP 1: In a large bowl, whisk the eggs and cold water to blend.

STEP 2: Add the levain, brown sugar, honey, orange zest, lemon zest, and vanilla and whisk until just incorporated.

STEP 3: Add the butter cubes, flours, and salt and mix as instructed using Mixing Dough: Method 2 (page 27) to finish working this dough. Knead for a good 10 to 15 minutes.

STEP 4: Cover the dough and let ferment at room temperature for 6 hours. Refrigerate the dough for 12 hours more.

To shape and proof the dough:

STEP 1: Line 2 sheet pans with parchment paper and set aside.

STEP 2: Turn the dough out on to a floured work surface, divide it into 50- to 100-g pieces (depending on the size you want your buns to be), and shape each piece using the balling up technique (see Shaping Dough: Method 3— Balling Up, page 31).

STEP 3: If you want your buns topped with seeds, use a pastry brush to coat the dough balls with water and then dip them onto a plate full of sesame or poppy seeds.

STEP 4: Arrange the buns on the prepared sheet pans, 3 by 4 for 100-g balls, or 4 by 5 for 50-g balls. You don't have to be perfect; they will still bake well if they touch during the bake.

STEP 5: Fill an ovenproof pot with boiling water and put it into the cold oven. With the oven off and cold, put your trays of buns inside the oven and let them proof for 3 hours.

(continued)

To bake the buns:

STEP 1: Remove the proofed buns and the pot from the oven.

STEP 2: Preheat the oven to 375°F (190°C).

STEP 3: Using a pastry brush, brush the buns with water. Bake the buns for 15 to 20 minutes until they are dark brown and have a shiny surface. Keep an eye on their progress and rotate the pans halfway through the baking time to ensure even coloring.

⚜ **TIP**: Store extra buns in the freezer after they have cooled completely. To re-use, simply toast them in a 350°F (180°C) oven for 5 minutes.

CUBAN MUFFINS

LEVAIN BUILD

- 60 g mature sourdough starter
- 120 g bread flour
- 110 g warm water

FINAL DOUGH MIX

- 250 g bread flour
- 250 g all-purpose flour
- 330 g warm water
- 150 g levain
- 65 g lard (see tip)
- 25 g light brown sugar
- 10 g salt
- Cornmeal, for dusting
- Semolina flour, for dusting

Can you guess how this recipe came about? Well, if you've ever confused dough because it's super early in the morning and you haven't had coffee, then you get me. There I am, thinking my English muffin dough is out; yet, when the dough hits the griddle I start to smell the beautifully acidic and fatty aroma of pan Cubano as if I was in the cafeteria about to order a *sanguich*. I was far from upset, though, for I knew immediately that the Cuban muffin was born. I laughed, cooked them all, and make some of the best breakfast Cuban *sanguiches* I've ever had.

———

To build the levain: In a tall jar or medium bowl, mix the mature starter, flour, and warm water until incorporated. Cover with a lid or clean kitchen towel and leave in a warm place for 3 to 4 hours, or until doubled in size. You can use your levain immediately, or you can refrigerate it for 12 hours to use later or the next day.

See Building and Maintaining a Levain (page 24) for more tips on how to tell if your levain is ready.

To make the final dough mix:

STEP 1: In a large bowl, mix the flours, water, levain, lard, brown sugar, and salt as instructed in Mixing Dough: Method 2 (page 27) until incorporated.

STEP 2: Cover the dough and let ferment at room temperature for 6 hours. Refrigerate the dough overnight for fermentation, or 8 to 10 hours.

To shape and proof the dough:

STEP 1: Line a sheet pan with parchment paper and dust the parchment with cornmeal and semolina flour. Set aside.

STEP 2: Place the dough on a floured work surface and flatten it into a rectangle about ¾ inch (2 cm) thick. Use a large (3- or 4-inch, or 7.5 or 10 cm) cup or round cookie cutter to cut the dough into about 8 disks. Transfer these to the prepared sheet pan.

STEP 3: Let the muffins proof for about 30 minutes and then cook them immediately.

To cook the muffins:

STEP 1: Heat a cast iron skillet over medium-low heat until hot.

STEP 2: Dust the skillet with corn meal and semolina. Add the muffins and cook for 4 to 5 minutes per side. This may vary depending on your stove.

STEP 3: Let cool for about 20 minutes to ensure that the inside is fully cooked before cutting. You can use a fork to poke them open, use a knife to cut them, or just bite into them. I've had success with all methods!

❧ **TIP**: For lard, I use any brand I can find in the grocery store, such as Goya. If you live in a place where lard is not easy to attain, simply use oil: vegetable, avocado, or grapeseed oil all work well.

JAMAICAN HARD DOUGH

LEVAIN BUILD

- 60 g mature sourdough starter
- 120 g bread flour
- 110 g warm water

FINAL DOUGH MIX

- 500 g bread flour
- 300 g water
- 110 g levain
- 50 g unsalted butter
- 20 g granulated sugar
- 8 g salt
- Oil, for preparing the pan

Although my dad was born and raised in Honduras, I was fascinated when I learned my grand-father was Jamaican. Since learning about this, I have had no choice but to explore and understand one of the most common breads you will find on the table in a Jamaican household—hard dough. This slightly sweet but dense table bread is perfect for moist sandwiches filled with fried eggs, plantains, or meats that need something more durable than your average pullman loaf. You can also use it on the table with your favorite sweet or savory spreads and toppings.

To build the levain: In a tall jar or medium bowl, mix the mature starter, flour, and warm water until incorporated. Cover with a lid or clean kitchen towel and leave in a warm place for 3 to 4 hours, or until doubled in size. You can use your levain immediately, or refrigerate it for 12 hours to use later or the next day.

See Building and Maintaining a Levain (page 24) for more tips on how to tell if your levain is ready.

To make the final dough mix:

STEP 1: In a large bowl, mix all the final dough mix ingredients as instructed using Mixing Dough: Method 2 (page 27) until incorporated.

STEP 2: Cover the dough and let ferment at room temperature for 4 hours.

To shape and proof the dough:

STEP 1: Coat a loaf tin with oil and set aside.

STEP 2: Turn the dough out on to a floured work surface and shape the dough using a tension roll (see Shaping Dough: Method 1— Tension Roll, page 28).

STEP 3: Place your shaped loaf in the prepared tin. Cover the dough and let proof at room temperature for 4 hours more.

To bake the bread:

STEP 1: Preheat the oven to 375°F (190°C).

STEP 2: Using a pastry brush, brush the loaf with water. Bake the bread for 20 to 25 minutes until golden brown on top.

MALLORCAS

LEVAIN BUILD

- 75 g mature sourdough starter
- 100 g bread flour
- 50 g whole-wheat flour
- 150 g warm water

FINAL DOUGH MIX

- 100 g eggs
- 100 g cold milk
- 200 g levain
- 100 g light brown sugar
- 5 g grated lemon zest
- 1 g vanilla extract
- 100 g unsalted butter, cubed
- 400 g bread flour
- 100 g all-purpose flour
- 6 g salt
- Boiling water, for proofing

FILLING AND TOPPING

- 50 g unsalted butter, at room temperature
- 5 g granulated sugar
- Powdered sugar, for topping

Before the trip with my friend to his native Puerto Rico, where I encountered some amazing Pan de Agua (page 65), I lived with him in college. I remember him receiving packages full of sweet rolls that he would eat almost every day until they were gone. Then he'd pick up the phone, dial up his family, and ask for more mallorcas, *por favor*!

I had never heard of these but I was extremely happy when he enlightened me. Mallorcas are an addictive, sweet, soft bread coated with powdered sugar and found at every bakery on the island of Puerto Rico. Historically, pan de mallorca is from Spain, but it can also be found in different Caribbean countries. They can be sliced in half and used for sandwiches, or eaten with jam and butter. Either way, you are guaranteed to eat more than one at a time.

––––––

To build the levain: In a tall jar or medium bowl, mix the mature starter, flours, and warm water until incorporated. Cover with a lid or clean kitchen towel and leave in a warm place for 3 to 4 hours. You can use your levain immediately, or refrigerate it for 12 hours to use later or the next day.

See Building and Maintaining a Levain (page 24) for more tips on how to tell if your levain is ready.

To make the final dough mix:

STEP 1: In a large bowl, whisk the eggs and cold milk to combine.

STEP 2: Add the levain, brown sugar, lemon zest, and vanilla. Whisk until just incorporated.

STEP 3: Add the cubed butter, flours, and salt. Mix the ingredients together using Mixing Dough: Method 2 (page 27) to finish working this dough.

STEP 4: Cover the dough and let ferment at room temperature for 6 hours. Refrigerate the dough for 12 hours more.

To shape, fill, and proof the dough:

STEP 1: Line a sheet pan with parchment paper and set aside.

STEP 2: Turn the dough out on to a floured work surface and pat it down and into a rectangle about 12 × 8 inches (30 × 20 cm).

STEP 3: From the filling ingredients, spread the room-temperature butter over the dough and evenly sprinkle the granulated sugar on top. Cut the rectangle horizontally into 12 (1-inch-, or 2.5 cm, wide) strips. Roll each strip into a pinwheel. Arrange the mallorca rolls on the prepared sheet pan with enough space between so they can grow. It's also okay if they touch during the bake.

STEP 4: Fill an ovenproof pot with boiling water and put it into the cold oven. With the oven off and cold, put your trays of mallorcas inside the oven and let them proof for 2 to 3 hours.

(continued)

To bake the mallorcas:

STEP 1: Remove the mallorcas and pot from the oven.

STEP 2: Preheat the oven to 375°F (190°C).

STEP 3: Using a pastry brush, brush the tops of the mallorcas with water. Bake the mallorcas for 20 minutes, or until light brown.

STEP 4: Sprinkle liberally with powdered sugar while warm.

MUFFALETTA ROLLS

LEVAIN BUILD

- 50 g mature sourdough starter
- 90 g bread flour
- 10 g whole-wheat flour
- 100 g warm water

FINAL DOUGH MIX

- 250 g bread flour
- 250 g all-purpose flour
- 315 g water
- 200 g levain
- 10 g granulated sugar
- 6 g salt
- 300 g sesame seeds

OLIVE SALAD MIX

- 125 g pimiento-stuffed olives, halved
- 125 g Kalamata olives, halved
- 30 g extra-virgin olive oil
- 3 garlic cloves, minced
- 5 g red pepper flakes
- 5 g dried oregano
- 5 g dried parsley
- 5 g diced shallot
- 5 g capers

When I was a kid, I'd eat olives from the fridge straight out of the jar. I'm so glad my love of olives led me to create a bread full of classic New Orleans–style muffaletta olive salad. This slightly spicy and texture-rich olive salad is used as a spread on muffaletta sandwiches, which usually come on a round sesame bun. We can keep the sesame on top, no problem, but the inside of the actual roll? You guessed it. Filled with delicious olive salad!

_____

To build the levain: In a tall jar or medium bowl, mix the mature starter, flours, and warm water until incorporated. Cover with a lid or clean kitchen towel and leave in a warm place for 3 to 4 hours, or until doubled in size. You can use your levain immediately, or refrigerate it for 12 hours to use later, or the next day.

See Building and Maintaining a Levain (page 24) for more tips on how to tell if your levain is ready.

To make the final dough mix:

In a large bowl, mix the flours, water, levain, granulated sugar, and salt. Don't work the dough too much, just ensure there is no dry flour remaining. Let rest for 30 minutes.

To make the olive salad mix:

While the dough rests, in a medium bowl, stir together the olive salad mix ingredients until you have a uniform mixture. Set aside.

To finish the final dough mix:

STEP 1: After the 30 minutes has elapsed, dump the dough out on to a work surface and lightly pat it down.

STEP 2: Spread half the muffaletta olive salad over the dough, then fold the dough in half. Spread half the remaining olive salad on the folded dough and fold it again. Put the dough back into the bowl and pour the remaining salad mixture over the top of the dough. Cover the dough and let rest for 30 minutes.

STEP 3: Dump out the dough one more time and perform the same stretches and folds from step 2. Try to ensure even distribution of the olive salad mixture. Put the dough back into the bowl, cover it, and let ferment at room temperature for 5 hours.

(continued)

To shape and proof the dough:

STEP 1: Line a sheet pan with parchment paper and set aside.

STEP 2: Turn the dough out on to a lightly floured surface, divide it into 100-g pieces (about 15), and shape each piece using the rounding technique (see Shaping Dough: Method 2—Rounding, page 30).

STEP 3: Pour the sesame seeds onto another sheet pan. Line a separate pan with a small, clean kitchen towel and pour water into the sheet pan.

STEP 4: Roll the top of each dough piece in the wet towel, then roll it in the sesame seeds. This will give the dough a nice coating of sesame seeds before the proof. Place the rolls on the prepared sheet pan, seed-side up.

STEP 5: Cover the rolls and refrigerate overnight, for 12 hours, or let sit at room temperature for 3 to 4 hours.

To bake the rolls:

STEP 1: Preheat the oven to 375°F (190°C).

STEP 2: Bake the rolls for 15 to 20 minutes, or until golden brown.

PÃO DE QUEIJO (CHEESE BREAD)

FINAL DOUGH MIX

- 100 g unsalted butter
- 1 garlic clove, minced
- 315 g tapioca or cassava flour
- 30 g whole-wheat flour
- 5 g salt
- 2 g red pepper flakes
- 1 egg
- 75 g mature sourdough starter
- 200 g water
- 100 g shredded Parmesan cheese
- 50 g shredded mozzarella cheese

Since I've lived in Miami, I've never found it hard to find a good pão de queijo (cheese bread in Portuguese). When I first bit into pão de queijo, I was surprised at how light and creamy it was. The melted cheese was divine and it got me thinking about whether this bread could be made with some wheat flour and sourdough starter. In Brazil, where wheat was not a resource at the time, pão de queijo was made in wood-burning ovens and was typically gluten free. Although this bread is not typically leavened, my goal of incorporating levain into this recipe is not to achieve volume, but to achieve and explore different flavor profiles. Either way, if you like to eat things with melted cheese warm out of the oven, this recipe is for you.

Note: There is no levain build for this recipe. What I want you to use is mature sourdough starter, that is, the starter you would typically feed to build a levain. See more information on page 23.

To make the final dough mix:

STEP 1: In a small saucepan over medium-low heat, combine the butter and garlic. Heat until the butter melts. Remove from the heat and let cool.

STEP 2: In a large bowl, combine the flours, salt, red pepper flakes. Pour in the cooled garlic butter mix until incorporated.

STEP 3: Add the egg and mature sourdough starter. Mix until incorporated. Add the cheeses and mix again to combine.

STEP 4: Cover the bowl and refrigerate the dough overnight, for 12 hours.

To shape the dough:

No need to proof these guys. They are ready to go straight into the preheated oven.

STEP 1: Preheat the oven to 400°F (200°C). Line a sheet pan with parchment paper and set aside.

STEP 2: Divide the dough into 10 pieces and shape each piece using the rounding technique (see Shaping Dough: Method 2—Rounding, page 30). No need to flour the work surface.

STEP 3: Place the rolls on the prepared sheet pan evenly spaced.

To bake the bread:

STEP 1: Place the rolls into the oven and drop the temperature to 375°F (190°C).

STEP 2: Bake for 15 to 20 minutes, or until golden brown.

PAN DE CAFÉ (COFFEE BREAD)

LEVAIN BUILD

- 50 g mature sourdough starter
- 50 g bread flour
- 50 g whole-wheat flour
- 90 g warm water

FINAL DOUGH MIX

- 500 g bread flour
- 100 g brewed coffee, chilled
- 215 g water
- 50 g unsalted butter, plus more for preparing the pan
- 30 g light brown sugar
- 100 g levain
- 8 g salt

FILLING

- 10 g ground cinnamon
- 10 g fresh coffee grounds
- 10 g granulated sugar

The two things in this world I cannot live without are coffee and bread. They are usually the first things I think about when I wake up, and before bed, I'm usually plotting where I'll have my morning coffee just to be sure. So I thought, why not get the best of both worlds? The goal of this loaf is to make something that is versatile yet not too sweet. This bread goes extremely well with peanut butter and fruit jams, as well as savory sandwiches like goat cheese and caramelized onion. If you love the essence of coffee, I strongly recommend using your favorite roast or coffee flavor.

———

To build the levain: In a tall jar or medium bowl, mix the mature starter, flours, and warm water until incorporated. Cover with a lid or clean kitchen towel and leave in a warm place for 3 to 4 hours, or until doubled in size. You can use your levain immediately, or refrigerate it for 12 hours to use later or the next day.

See Building and Maintaining a Levain (page 24) for more tips on how to tell if your levain is ready.

To make the final dough mix:

STEP 1: In a large bowl, mix all the final dough mix ingredients as instructed in Mixing Dough: Method 2 (page 27) until incorporated.

STEP 2: Cover the dough and let rest at room temperature for 4 hours. Refrigerate the dough overnight, 8 to 10 hours.

To shape and proof the dough:

Turn the dough out on to a floured work surface and let rest at room temperature for 30 minutes.

To make the filling:

While the dough rests, in a small bowl, stir together the cinnamon, coffee, and granulated sugar. Set aside.

To finish shaping and proofing the dough:

STEP 1: Coat a loaf tin with butter and set aside.

STEP 2: Pat down the dough into a square. Spread the filling in a thin, even layer over the dough.

STEP 3: Roll the dough into a tight log using the tension roll technique (see Shaping Dough: Method 1—Tension Roll, page 28) and place it in the prepared tin.

STEP 4: Cover the dough and let proof for 3 hours.

To bake the bread:

STEP 1: Preheat the oven to 375°F (190°C).

STEP 2: Using a pastry brush, brush the top of the loaf with water.

STEP 3: Bake the bread for 30 to 35 minutes, or until golden brown.

"A LIGHT BROWN CRUST THAT SHATTERS, A SOFT BUT CHEWY INTERIOR, AND A SUBTLE FLAVOR THAT DOESN'T OVERPOWER YOUR SANDWICH."

QUEEN CAKE

LEVAIN BUILD

- 75 g mature sourdough starter
- 125 g bread flour
- 25 g whole-wheat flour
- 150 g warm water

FINAL DOUGH MIX

- 330 g eggs
- 200 g milk, plus more for brushing
- 200 g levain
- 3 g vanilla extract
- 500 g all-purpose flour
- 450 g bread flour
- 50 g whole-wheat flour
- 340 g granulated sugar, divided
- 330 g unsalted butter, at room temperature (not melted)
- 18 g salt
- 25 g ground cinnamon, divided
- 5 g ground nutmeg
- Zest of 1 orange
- Zest of 1 lemon
- 20 g melted unsalted butter

FILLING

- 100 g powdered sugar
- 100 g cream cheese, at room temperature
- 100 g raspberry jam
- 100 g pineapple jam

ICING

- 200 g cream cheese, at room temperature
- 150 g powdered sugar
- 5 g freshly squeezed lemon juice

What's better than a king cake? Well, how about one that is souped up with every type of delicious filling imaginable? Many bakeries in New Orleans offer their version of a queen cake and I'd like to offer you mine. My queen cake is a naturally leavened, cinnamon-sugar brioche-style bread formed into a ring and stuffed with a variety of flavors. However, feel free to add whichever fillings you like most. From homemade jams to fresh fruit and pastry creams, your queen cake can—and should—have it all.

———

To build the levain: In a tall jar or medium bowl, mix the mature starter, flours, and warm water until incorporated. Cover with a lid or clean kitchen towel and leave in a warm place for 3 to 4 hours, or until doubled in size. You can use your levain immediately, or refrigerate for 12 hours to use later or the next day.

See Building and Maintaining a Levain (page 24) for more tips on how to tell if your levain is ready.

To make the final dough mix:

STEP 1: In a large bowl, whisk the eggs, milk, levain, and vanilla until incorporated.

STEP 2: Add the flours, 330 g of granulated sugar, the room-temperature butter, salt, 15 g of cinnamon, the nutmeg, orange zest, and lemon zest. Mix the ingredients as instructed in Mixing Dough: Method 2 (page 27) until incorporated.

STEP 3: Cover the dough and let ferment at room temperature for 6 hours. Transfer the dough to the refrigerator for 12 hours of fermentation.

To shape and proof the dough:

STEP 1: Line a sheet pan with parchment paper and set aside.

STEP 2: Turn the dough out on to a floured work surface, punch it down, and form the dough into a rectangle. Brush the dough with melted butter and sprinkle with the remaining 10 g of cinnamon and 10 g of granulated sugar.

STEP 3: Starting at one of the long ends, roll the dough into a log and form the log into an oval with the tips meeting. Place the dough oval on the prepared sheet pan.

STEP 4: Cover the dough and let proof at room temperature for 3 to 4 hours, or until puffy.

(continued)

To bake the queen cake:

STEP 1: Preheat the oven to 375°F (190°C).

STEP 2: Using a pastry brush, coat the dough with milk.

STEP 3: Bake the cake for 35 to 40 minutes, or until golden brown.

STEP 4: Let the cake cool completely before filling.

To make the filling:

If you like your stuffed cakes on the really filled side, feel free to double or even triple the amount of filling ingredients.

STEP 1: Using a small kitchen knife, poke several holes in the completely cooled cake bottom, all around the oval, for the filling.

STEP 2: In a medium bowl, whisk together the powdered sugar and cream cheese until creamy. Transfer to a pastry bag, or resealable plastic bag and snip off a bottom corner.

STEP 3: Place the raspberry jam and pineapple jam each in a separate pastry bag, or resealable plastic bag and snip off a bottom corner from each.

STEP 4: To fill the cake, insert the pastry bags into the holes and squeeze in the filling. I like to alternate fillings (cream cheese in one, raspberry jam in the next, pineapple jam next, etc.).

To make the icing:

STEP 1: In a small bowl, whisk the cream cheese, powdered sugar, and lemon juice until creamy.

STEP 2: Spread the icing all over the top of the filled cake.

WHOLE-GRAIN PINEAPPLE CREAM BEIGNETS

YIELD: 16 TO 20 FILLED BEIGNETS, DEPENDING ON SIZE

LEVAIN BUILD

- 50 g mature sourdough starter
- 50 g bread flour
- 50 g whole-wheat flour
- 85 g warm water

FINAL DOUGH MIX

- 400 g bread flour
- 110 g levain
- 100 g whole-wheat flour, plus more for dusting
- 200 g whole milk
- 100 g water
- 80 g light brown sugar
- 50 g unsalted butter
- 2 eggs
- 6 g salt
- 1 g vanilla extract
- 1½ L vegetable oil, or canola oil
- Lots of powdered sugar, for dusting

PINEAPPLE CREAM

- 453 g whole milk
- 113 g heavy cream
- 113 g egg yolks
- 57 g granulated sugar
- 40 g cornstarch
- 3 g vanilla bean paste
- 100 g crushed pineapple, or puréed pineapple

Having beignets is a magical experience. They are light, slightly crispy, and sweet. But one day, I decided I wanted to take my beignets to the next level. I wanted to incorporate a reasonable percentage of whole-grain flour to play around with a new flavor profile and textures in this sweet treat. I also realized I have never had a stuffed beignet. My first instinct was to reach for a coconut, as usual, but I decided to switch it up and use pineapple to add a slight tartness to balance the sweet powdered sugar. Rest assured that there is now a new, classic beignet on the block. Grab the café au lait.

———

To build the levain: In a tall jar or bowl, mix the mature starter, flours, and warm water until incorporated. Cover the jar with a lid or clean kitchen towel and leave in a warm place for 3 to 4 hours, or until doubled in size. You can use your levain immediately, or refrigerate it for 12 hours to use later or the next day.

See Building and Maintaining a Levain (page 24) for more tips on how to tell if your levain is ready.

To make the final dough mix:

STEP 1: In a large bowl, combine the levain, flour, milk, water, brown sugar, butter, eggs, salt, and vanilla and mix until incorporated and no flour remains. Using Mixing Dough: Method 2 (page 27), work the dough and knead it until you have a smooth surface.

STEP 2: Cover the dough and let sit at room temperature for 6 hours. Transfer to the refrigerator overnight, or for 8 to 10 hours.

To make the pineapple cream:

STEP 1: In a medium saucepan over medium-high heat, whisk the milk, heavy cream, egg yolks, granulated sugar, cornstarch, and vanilla bean paste to combine. Bring the mixture to a boil.

STEP 2: Once boiling, remove from the heat, add the pineapple, and whisk vigorously until creamy. Pour the pineapple cream into a medium bowl and place plastic wrap over it. Refrigerate overnight.

To shape and proof the dough:

STEP 1: Line a sheet pan with parchment paper and set aside.

STEP 2: Turn the dough out on to a floured work surface, pat it down, and form it into a rectangle. Using a pizza cutter or a large chef's knife, cut the dough into 16 to 20 squares.

STEP 3: Place the dough squares on the prepared sheet pan. Let proof for 30 minutes, or until the cooking oil gets up to temperature.

(continued)

To cook the beignets:

STEP 1: Fill a large bowl with powdered sugar. You will use this to toss your beignets in after they are out of the fryer.

STEP 2: In a large pot over medium-high heat, bring the vegetable oil to about 350°F (180°C). If you do not have a thermometer to measure the oil's temperature, let the oil get so hot you can see a bit of smoke rising from it and then turn it down to a simmer until the heat subsides.

STEP 3: Working in batches, as needed, add the beignets to the hot oil and fry them for 3 minutes per side, using a heat-resistant utensil to flip them.

STEP 4: Transfer the hot beignets to the powdered sugar and shake the bowl so they get completely covered. Transfer the sugared beignets to a paper towel–lined plate and let cool completely.

To fill the beignets:

STEP 1: Transfer the pineapple cream into a piping bag or resealable plastic bag, and snip off a bottom corner.

STEP 2: At the corner or tip of each beignet, use a knife to poke a hole all the way into the center. Insert your pastry tip and fill as desired.

STEP 3: Get yourself a napkin, sit down with a café au lait, and enjoy!

RESOURCES

Tools and Ingredients

When baking at home in the United States, I find the best places to go for my baking needs are Whole Foods and Amazon. You can get a variety of ingredients and tools from both retailers. Amazon is a great place to find different flour types, such as spelt flour.

I often use King Arthur organic flour for my bakes, as it is a high-quality flour and is affordable in small quantities. If you can find a bakery supply warehouse in your city, it is possible you'll be able to buy big bags of flour at wholesale prices. You'll have to drive around or search online to find one.

Reading Material

I am always inspired by books, magazines, and social media accounts, such as *Bread* by Jeffrey Hamelman and *Bake from Scratch Magazine*. If you search for #sourdough on your social media accounts, you can find a variety of information related to making sourdough bread.

About the Author

BRYAN FORD is a bread baker from New Orleans who is known for experimenting with baking techniques while infusing his passion and Latin American culture into his recipes on his popular blog, www.artisanbryan.com, and Instagram, @artisanbryan. Viewed in over 100 countries, the Artisan Bryan blog won the 2019 *Saveur* magazine award for Best Baking and Sweets Blog. Ford is especially known for his sourdough pan de coco recipe, inspired by a traditional Honduran bread. Bryan is currently a recipe consultant for bakeries in the United States and Central America.

ACKNOWLEDGMENTS

Nothing has ever been more important to me than my family, roots, and upbringing. I would not be able to pursue my passions without all of you! I love you all!

To my mother, Herling Madrid:

My inspiration and motivation, who raised me with kindness, joy, and so much love. I have still never tasted better food than yours and have never seen anyone work harder to achieve their goals. Thank you for believing in me as I try to achieve my goals! With every challenge I face, I remember the challenges you have already overcome.

To my father, Glen Ford:

You supported every hobby and dream I had and always gave me positive encouragement to keep pushing forward. You taught me how to hustle and work odd jobs to keep myself afloat, and you always inspired me to follow my heart.

To my wife, Alycia Domma:

Some people say better half, soulmate, or support system but, the truth is, you are my everything. I would be completely lost and unable to be my true self without you. It is only fitting that this book will be published in our tenth year together, ten beautiful years that are full of adventures, love, good times, and good food. Thank you for putting up with all the flour and dough that I miss when I clean!

To my siblings, Lizzie Ford-Madrid, Glen Ford, and Ariana Ford:

We ain't even supposed to be here! I miss watching our favorite movies, eating our favorite foods, and playing our favorite games together. Even though we have grown so much in age and experience, I always feel like little Bryan trying to steal *baleadas* off your plates! I'm so proud of how each of you has worked so hard to open new doors in your life. I love and miss you guys so much.

To my friends, new and old:

I've known you guys in different ways and at different times in my life. You have each added special value to my existence, talking with me when times are tough and laughing with me when the good times are rolling. Forget the tough stuff anyway, *laissez les bon temps rouler*!

Index